GLOBAL UX

GLOBAL UX
Design and Research in a Connected World

WHITNEY QUESENBERY
and DANIEL SZUC

with Sketchnotes by
AMANDA WRIGHT

AMSTERDAM • BOSTON • HEIDELBERG • LONDON • NEW YORK • OXFORD
PARIS • SAN DIEGO • SAN FRANCISCO • SINGAPORE • SYDNEY • TOKYO
Morgan Kaufmann is an imprint of Elsevier

Acquiring Editor: Rachel Roumeliotis
Development Editor: Dave Bevans
Project Manager: Jessica Vaughan
Designer: Joanne Blank

Morgan Kaufmann is an imprint of Elsevier
225 Wyman Street, Waltham, MA 02451, USA

Library of Congress Cataloging-in-Publication Data
Quesenbery, Whitney.
  Global UX : design and research in a connected world / Whitney Quesenbery, Daniel Szuc.
     p. cm.
  Includes index.
  ISBN 978-0-12-378591-6
  1. Product design. 2. Consumers—Research. 3. New products—Cross-cultural studies.
4. Marketing—Cross-cultural studies. I. Szuc, Daniel. II. Title.
  TS171.Q38 2012
  658.5′752—dc23
                                                                    2011032825

British Library Cataloguing-in-Publication Data
A catalogue record for this book is available from the British Library.

ISBN: 978-0-12-378591-6

Printed in the United States of America
12 13 14 15 16   10 9 8 7 6 5 4 3 2 1

Working together to grow
libraries in developing countries

www.elsevier.com | www.bookaid.org | www.sabre.org

ELSEVIER   BOOK AID International   Sabre Foundation

For information on all MK publications visit our website at www.mkp.com

Dedication

To JoBot, the Wookie, and Smudge

CONTENTS

FOREWORD

This book asks something of you beyond learning, beyond understanding of a few new methods, beyond cultural sensitivity. Read seriously, for it challenges you to move your center of attention outside yourself, to see and hear without your familiar and very comfortable lenses, filters, and judgments. It asks you to be open to the possibility that some of your deep underlying assumptions—those things you assume to be universally true—might not hold true for everyone in every place.

To say it another way, this book asks you to make a professional practice of changing how you see yourself and your place in the world (and by "you," I mean you as an individual, or collectively your team, your project, or your company). To successfully apply the advice and approaches described in this book, you have to become someone who is capable of applying them with an open mind and an open heart.

In my experience, that is exactly what is required to be a competent designer or strategist in any context or role in the cloud of practices surrounding the term "User Experience." If you rely on your own past, your own skills, competencies, beliefs and preferred solutions, you deny yourself and all the businesses and people you serve the possibility of what can happen when your cumulative experience meets the miraculous variety and depth of the world.

There are powerful enemies that conspire to keep you from that possibility.

Working from outside: Most of us are trained to believe that we can stand outside a situation, create something, inject it into the lives of the people who dwell inside that situation, and reliably have that new thing be appropriate, desirable, and "good." Decades of attempts demonstrate the unreliability and dangers of this belief. The antidote is to work from inside the situation. Let go of the need to be an "expert," work alongside the people who live the situation every day and let the new thing be born through that collaboration.

"Us/Them" mentality: If you focus on the differences between yourself and the people who will use the results of your work, you cheat yourself and your organization. This can be a very subtle, well-disguised form of arrogance. It damages your ability to learn from their world, understand deeply, and create that thing that you will never conceive unless you find the connections that turn "us/them" into "we."

Fear: Difference is scary. It can be uncomfortable to encounter a different culture, but it can be downright frightening to let go of everything you think you know and make room for strangeness inside yourself and your team. It requires an act of vulnerability, of embracing the possibility that you might be changed through your work. In my experience, once you notice the fear and start talking about it—putting it out in front of you and asking where it comes from—it shrinks from the exposure. Fear can't stand the open air. Then you're free to mix your deep capabilities with the deep unknown and create something new and truly fitting.

As the authors explicitly mention, this book goes to press in a time when businesses and design professionals are revisiting the purpose of their work. In many circles, the tone of conversation is shifting from "I" to "We" and from "sell/acquire more stuff" to "foster more quality of life." As a measure of value, "Life" is rising in prominence over "Growth." Innovation for its own sake is becoming less valuable than the work of discovering latent positive possibilities and finding ways to strengthen and amplify their progress.

It is difficult enough to do such work within one's home culture. As a society, we have yet to master that practice. Still, an increasing number of people are finding themselves faced with the even more difficult challenge of creating positive outcomes for life and business across global cultures. The task is humbling.

So thank you, Whitney and Dan, for this collection of experience, wisdom, approach, and advice to help us with our work.

Marc Rettig

September 2011
Pittsburgh

ACKNOWLEDGEMENTS

When we set out to write this book, it was something entirely different than what it has become. Instead of a book of business case studies, we have a collection of stories about people's lives and UX practice.

That is not a book we could ever have written alone. Its strength is in the overlapping experiences we heard from literally dozens of people. The list of the people we formally interviewed for this book follows these acknowledgements. In the quotes throughout the book, we briefly identify the person speaking, but the short bios at the back of the book will let you read their thoughts in a broader context.

In addition to those formal interviews, we also had even more informal conversations with people as we worked on projects, attended conferences, or chatted on Twitter and the many UX sites and e-mail lists.

We have to thank Paul Sherman because he started us on this journey. We missed him when work, life, and family drew him away.

Ani Moriarty did the transcriptions for many of the interviews. Amanda Wright didn't even hesitate when we wrote to her out of the blue and asked her to do the amazing sketchnotes that end each chapter.

Jhumkee Iyengar, Gerry Gaffney, Carol Barnum, and Ginny Redish read some of the rough chapters, patiently giving us amazing comments that helped shape this book.

All of the contributors got to read a near-final draft. Their reactions gave us hope that it would all come together in the end, and their comments helped us fine-tune the manuscript.

Calvin Chan helped with some of the illustrations. Donna Spencer and Steve "Doc" Baty accepted a presentation for UX Australia 2011 when we were still trying to figure out what would go in the book.

Both of us have met many people around the world through our work on the board of the Usability Professionals' Association (UPA), though at different times. Silvia Zimmermann, Jason Huang, and Denny Huang's work to make UPA more global was an inspiration for us.

Our families did what families do and gave us all the encouragement and support we could hope for. Whitney, however, still hopes to collect on some of those great dumpling dinners that Dan tweets about so often on his way home. Dr. Ken, Van and Siu Bo, Dr. Kwok, and Hok Wong also helped Dan keep body and soul together. John Chester kept the lights on and wireless running for Whitney.

In Dan's peripatetic life, Matthew Oliphant and family, and Matt Wallens and Amanda Nance both provided a temporary home.

Our colleagues also inspired us on the journey—Sarah Bloomer, Sonya Chik, Ian Fenn, Lisa Halabi, Caroline Jarrett, Sheryl Lumb, Perry Offer, John Philpin, Jay Rogers, Keith Smith, Simon Spencer, Jared Spool, and Lisa Welchman.

The folks at Morgan Kauffman did all the good things that publishers do. Mary James didn't blink when we announced that we wanted to completely change the concept for the book. Rachel Roumeliotis, Dave Bevans, Steve Elliott, and Jessica Vaughn saw it through.

Finally, our projects, notably Rob Findlay and the CX team in Singapore, our friends at Foolproof in the UK and HeathWallace in Hong Kong, the global organization of IEEE, The Open University in the UK, and the team at the National Cancer Institute all helped us think through what it means to be global.

ABOUT THE AUTHORS

Whitney Quesenbery

Whitney is a user researcher, user experience practitioner, and usability expert with a passion for clear communication. Her projects include work for the National Cancer Institute (US), The Open University (UK) and IEEE (worldwide). She enjoys learning about people and using those insights to products where people matter.

Pursuing her interest in the usability of civic life, she has served on two US government advisory committees: updating US "Section 508" accessibility regulations and creating standards US elections. She was president of the Usability Professionals' Association (UPA) International, on the board of the Center for Plain Language, and is a Fellow of the Society for Technical Communications.

Whitney is the author, with Kevin Brooks of *Storytelling for User Experience: Crafting stories for better design* (Rosenfeld Media, 2010). She's also proud that her chapter "Dimensions of Usability" in *Content and Complexity* turns up on so many course reading lists.

Currently lives: United States
WQusability: www.WQusability.com
Twitter @whitneyq

Daniel Szuc

Daniel is Principal Consultant at Apogee, a usability consulting Services Company based in Hong Kong.

Dan previously worked on a usability team for Telstra Australia. He is currently VP of the International UPA (Usability Professionals' Association) and has lectured about UX in Hong Kong, China, Singapore, Malaysia, Australia, the USA, Israel, New Zealand, and Japan.

He co-wrote a "Usability Kit" with Gerry Gaffney which is an implementation guide providing best practices and guidelines for usability teams. Dan holds a BS in Information Management from Melbourne University in Australia.

Currently lives: Hong Kong
Apogee: www.apogeehk.com
Twitter: @dszuc

Amanda Wright

Originally from Australia, although now a dual Australian-British citizen, Amanda lives in East London with her husband. She currently works for RMA Consulting. Prior to joining RMA, she worked on Yahoo! Answers. She loves to sketchnote and can often be found at conferences or talks sketching away.

When she's not working, she loves traveling, art, cooking, and trying to learn Mandarin Chinese. Her favorite method of transport is her Lemond Fillmore single speed bike or a London double-decker bus.

Currently lives: United Kingdom
Twitter: @yahnyinlondon
Web: www.yahnyinlondon.com

CONTRIBUTORS

This book is made possible by the many people who generously spent time to talk with us about their projects and professional practice.

We looked for people who live and work around the world … and we found them.

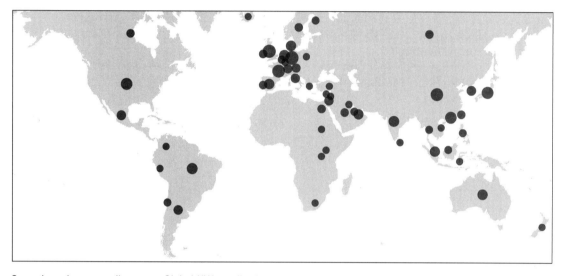

Countries where contributors to *Global UX* have lived or worked. Thanks to Calvin Chan for this data visualization.

The group currently lives in 14 different countries, but have—collectively—lived or worked on projects in more than 60. Some are obvious locations for UX work in North America, Europe, Asia, and South America. Some are less frequent destinations for UX projects: Sudan, Rwanda, Luxembourg, Cyprus, Iceland, and Peru, for example.

We speak 25 languages. Everyone speaks English. Daniel's native language is Australian English; Whitney's is US English, and it's the language of this book. Anne Kaikkonen leads the league table with five languages, but several people speak four and the average is two.

Peter Ballard
Robert Barlow-Busch
Steve Baty
Ronnie Battista
Jakob Biesterfeldt
Sarah Bloomer
Kevin Brooks
Andy Budd
Jennifer Carey
Samir Chabukswar
Raven Chai
Calvin Chan
Kevin Cheng
Giles Colborne
Jenna Date
Bill DeRouchey
Janna DeVylder
Wei Ding
Matt Dooley
Darci Dutcher
Jeff Eddings
Hsin Eu
Will Evans
Henning Fischer

Pabini Gabriel-Petit
Gerry Gaffney
Peter Grierson
Rachel Hinman
Adrian Hallam
Jim Hudson
Jhumkee Iyengar
Jhilmil Jain
Kaleem Khan
Anne Kaikkonen
Anjali Kelkar
Silvia LaHong
Mike Lai
Kevin Lee
Joe Leech
Yu-Hsiu Li
Tim Loo
Aaron Marcus
Chris Marmo
Itamar Medeiros
Trent Mankelow
Jim Nieters
Noriko Osaka
Christine Petersen

Martin Polley
Dennis Kei Yip Poon
Steve Portigal
Maren Pyenson
Bas Raijmakers
Michael de Regt
Katharina Reinecke
Marc Rettig
Chris Rourke
Josh Seiden
Tomer Sharon
Maria Sit
Vicky Teinaki
Geke van Dijk
Michele Visciola
Doug Wang
Mark Webster
Kimberly Wiessner
Jo Wong
Amanda Wright

THE START OF THE JOURNEY

IN THIS CHAPTER

It's 7 AM in California. Jim is on his second call of the morning planning a usability test in Israel. In the United Kingdom, Ian is in the middle of his day, which will include checking in with project teams in Saudi Arabia, Germany, and Argentina. In India, Deepa is getting ready to go out for some food before an evening call with colleagues in the United States.

Those are just a few snippets based on stories we gathered in interviews about working in global UX (user experience) with more than 65 UX practitioners, who have lived or worked in almost as many countries.

The important thing is that these events can and do happen anywhere. Travel used to be exotic. International travel for business was unusual. Even with the rise of multinational companies, most products and certainly most services were local.

Then the Internet happened, and it now it's hard to find anyone whose work isn't global in some way. Global teams collaborate around the world, among many countries, and in many configurations. And companies making digital products from e-commerce to games and social media do business across the world as easily as across the street. Even start-ups have global strategies.

Do we really think this is a new, more connected world? Actually, we do. For one thing, global work and travel are becoming routine. Here's what we heard from one person after another. "When I started working, the idea of working with a team in another country was sort of exotic and now it's just part of everyday practice." Think about how fast this has happened.

We're pretty lucky to be working at a time when you can routinely work with people all around the world, with projects and customers that are spread across many locations in a virtual network.

All this *global-ness* doesn't happen by accident, however. We talked to the people who make it happen. Our goal in this book is to show how good UX work is changing products around the world for the better. We have tried to look forward to what we can learn about tomorrow's UX practice from the leading trends today. You may find these glimpses into global practice are a mirror, reflecting your own work. You may find they are a beacon, showing a path ahead. Either way, we hope this book will inspire you and your own practice.

Before we get too far, let's define what we mean by "global work." Some people asked who or what had to be "global" to qualify and suggested choices that include:

- A group of (for example) Americans who work on a project for or in another country
- A group of people from many countries who work on a project for users in a single country, such as India
- Partners from several different countries who work together
- A global company that has people from all over the world
- Work on products or services used in more than one country

Our answer was, "Yes, all of those." We are interested in how people think about their work and all the global aspects of it.

This Book Is about People

As we started this book, our focus was on stories of successful projects. As we talked to many people in the field (and used up packs of sticky notes sorting out what we heard), the most compelling insights were not the case studies, the details of their methodology, or a specific business success. The interesting stories were about how they experienced the practice itself.

We listened to the data. As a result this book is about how user experience practice is changing and how practitioners and teams around the world are creating great user experiences for a global context. It's about the *how* more than the *what*.

This book is based on interviews with practitioners from many different countries, who work on many different types of projects. We looked behind the scenes at what it takes to create a user experience that works across borders, cultures, and languages.

We got input from a diverse group. We selected people for the interviews through a mix of planning, convenience, and snowball referrals. We looked for people who worked in different places, different industries, in a range of roles and UX disciplines, and with a variety of personal backgrounds.

We were especially interested in people who have worked in more than one country and people who have reached across cultures in their personal and professional lives. Some have lived in several countries for extended periods of time or have moved permanently to a new place. Some have jobs and projects that take them around the globe on a regular basis, while others travel more virtually.

The list of people who contributed to this book is just after the preface, and short biographies for each person are at the end of the book. In addition to many informal conversations, we recorded over 70 hours of interviews. Their thoughts on the challenges of the day-to-day work, as well as the larger issues of global UX, give this book a richer texture and more viewpoints than just those of two authors.

Like any ethnography or work of journalism, people are pictured in this book through their stories, their quotes, and what we learned by talking to them. But these portraits represent more than just the individuals. They are, we hope, enough of a collective voice that each of you reading this will see some part of yourself in them.

Charting the Territory

A few big themes emerged from these interviews. You will hear them reflected throughout the book, but they are important enough to mention right up front.

A Passion for User Experience

Even more than wanting diversity in the interviews, we wanted to talk to people with a passion for their work. And that passion came through over and over. We heard the same level of engaged innovation applied to work on a 25-year-old software product as to cutting edge start-ups.

In *The Power of Pull,* John Hagel III, John Seely Brown, and Lang Davison examined the shift to a networked knowledge economy and the "disposition"—the attitudes, world views, and behaviors—that make people successful in this shifting environment. In their view, workers who are passionate are inspired by unexpected challenges and energized by new problems to solve. These are the people who use their connections to explore ideas that lead to large and small innovations.

In our interviews, that passion came through clearly. For Jenna Date, the Director of the Masters in Human-Computer Interaction at Carnegie Mellon University, it sounded like this:

> I love doing work in different cultures just because it feels like it tests my edges and broadens my horizons as a human being as well as a researcher, and it gives me all of those experiences that I'm looking for in such a way that it tests me.
>
> **Jenna Date**

Or like this from Steve Baty, a principal at Meld Studios in Australia:

> When you start designing outside of your own cultural foundation, you have to really pay attention. If you are not open to those insights, you will just miss the opportunity to connect with the person you are designing for. Our design work is about creating a deep-seated emotional connection with people.
>
> **Steve (Doc) Baty**

There were dozens of different ways in which UX is focused on building bridges to connect cultures in large and small ways. We were also struck by how passionate people are about what their work means for our products, companies, and the world.

mrjoe Today I have calls with Munich, Madrid, Singapore, Hong Kong, Washington DC, Rio and Moscow.
6:32 AM Feb 18th

Figure 1.1 Days like this are not unusual for UX-ers working on several global projects at once. Joe Leech, User Experience Director, cxpartners @mrjoe, Twitter.

A Global UX Toolkit

We also learned that the toolkit of UX techniques is very consistent in practice around the world. This broad UX practice informs and is informed by the challenges of global UX.

Whether the story was about early user or design research to create a better understanding of the context, the challenges of bringing that cultural knowledge home, or insights into innovative design processes the basic techniques we heard about were similar. From ethnographic research to design ideation to usability testing, they all focused on similar ways to listen, observe, and learn.

We've taken a broad approach to the words that describe the activities of UX. To describe their work, people talked about
- User research, design research, and customer studies
- Field work, site visits, and research studies
- Interviews, sessions, and meetings, visits
- Customers, users, audience, participants, and people
- Countries, regions, and markets

Sometimes the words are an indication of their background or the kind of work they do, but it could also simply be the word they chose for that moment. English is not the first language for many of the people we spoke to, so there is that variable as well.

Rather than enforce our own definitions, we have tried to preserve each person's choices in both direct quotations and our descriptions. We hope that the variations in words add texture, not confusion.

This is also not a book about how to conduct international user research. Robert Schumacher's *The Handbook of Global User Research* is an excellent resource if you are looking for help with the details of running a user research project in several countries.

Global UX Perspectives

Any collaboration takes work and being a global team takes even more work. But that is the challenge of global UX. Time zones, different languages, communication styles, and problems in gaining access to users don't go away because we wish them to. When work is distributed across teams with different cultures, economic conditions, and time zones it is that much more difficult to stay focused on user needs and carry out high-quality design and design validation. But it isn't impossible.

UX starts with understanding the users, but it's not enough to just do a quick usability test or a few interviews, ticking off an item on a list by rote. We learned that doing user research right means putting your assumptions on the table and doing the work to either support or debunk them. It means taking the time to be open, to listen for the nuances of cultural perspectives. And it means helping all team members understand the messages of the research.

But even after the research sessions and feedback meetings are over, you need the diverse perspectives that bringing together a global team gives you, and ways to make sure that those voices are heard. It takes a long time, perhaps a whole lifetime, to really understand a culture, so teams need local voices to contribute to global projects.

Innovation from Everywhere

We also heard a lot of stories that suggest a fundamental change within some large corporations. Instead of all decisions coming from central headquarters, people and offices around the world are starting to have more influence.

When we removed the specific details and looked at the underlying pattern, that story went something like this:

> When he was first hired as a regional manager, the headquarters in the United States decided what he would sell in the region, and how he would sell it.

> Time passed, and now he was still told what to sell, but now asked to help decide how to sell it.

> More time passed. Now HQ asked what products would be successful in their market, and the regions built their own portfolios to meet local needs.

Recently, there has been another shift. Now the company is looking to the region to find ideas for new products that will meet local needs (and also be good for people in other parts of the world).

This change in the relationship can't come soon enough for people working in *the regions*. Everyone deserves a share of what Jhumkee Iyengar, a UX consultant based in India, calls the *thinking work*. More importantly, companies and their products will provide a better user experience for all.

Moving Into the Future

The stories we heard suggested that UX is continuing to make inroads. This is not to say that every company "gets it," but many do. As the saying goes, the future is unevenly applied, with some companies more solidly in the future than others.

As Jeff Eddings, a product manager at StumbleUpon, told us, "You can't do product management without user experience. The way the user interacts with your product, the goal you want the user to achieve … that's product management." This thought was echoed by Matt Dooley, Head of Digital Experiences from the global bank HSBC.

> Business managers today are expected to sieve through masses of essentially worthless data in the hope of discovering some insights and trends that will increase the value of the organization. So it's important to spend time up front to define a clear business strategy and what customer journeys and actions define business success. UX research and design is critical to the process of defining, refining, and validating what your customers really want. If you cut out user research, you may speed up the initial development process but I've found that it slows down the overall time to implement, as you don't have the customer insight and data to drive broad support and alignment for implementation. We have come a long way since the early 2000s, when we would frequently get design suggestions from senior management based on their own personal tastes and even comments passed to them by wives and friends on the design, color, and layout of specific pages.
>
> **Matt Dooley**

Or as Creative Director Kimberly Wiessner, also from HSBC said, "Having UX be part of leading the direction of the business through design is a huge transformational shift in our organization within the past four years. Who could say no to customers raving about a design vision?"

We know that your mileage may vary. You may be way out in a cutting edge environment for UX. You may be still trying to convince your company to take UX seriously. Either way, we hope you will find information here that resonates with you.

A Map of the Journey

Like the signpost on the cover of the book, the journey in this book starts "here" and points to many possible destinations. One of the standard disclaimers in a usability test is that "there is no right or wrong answer." That applies here as well. You, your team, and your company may start at different points on this journey, or may be interested in some parts more than others.

- Chapters 2 and 3 start with a quick look at the world outside of UX. This includes the external forces of change and globalization that affect us all and shape the context of our work as well as an overview of how culture affects both our practice and the user experience of the products we create.
- Chapters 4, 5, and 6 focus on what global UX means for an individual practitioner, a company, and our teams. We explore what it means to "think globally" or to "think locally" and the challenges that we have to address to work effectively in a bigger, flatter, more connected world.
- Chapters 7, 8, and 9 dive into details of global UX with the process and practice of research in the field, how we bring what we have learned home and share it with our colleagues, and how we use it in our designs.
- We end at Chapter 10 with some thoughts about how we deliver value both to our projects and the people for whom we ultimately work: the users of those products.

Through all of these pages, we have tried to look at all the levels of meaning as we think about both company and products on the one hand and people and culture on the other.

We should also say right up front that this is not a book specifically about the technical approaches for software. Localization and internationalization are critical, and we will look at how they fit into global UX, but our book has no charts showing how dates are written in countries around the world and no lists of rules for name order or formatting of addresses.

We hope that this book will give you some insights into how your colleagues have tackled the challenges of working on global products and designing for many cultures. The answers, however, will have to come from you as you consider yourself, your company, your team, your products, and your audience.

IT'S A NEW WORLD

IN THIS CHAPTER

UX is shaped by the same social, economic, business, and cultural forces that affect us as individuals. Many characteristics of the old world are vanishing as the world economy changes and as new technologies mature. We will be focusing on UX, but even within our own domain, it's not hard to see the evidence of a real shift.

Every time we read an article about trends in globalization, we can see echoes of its impact in our own experience and in stories we've heard from friends and colleagues.

In this chapter, we'll review some of the big trends that are changing the practice of UX:

- **The world is both smaller and larger.** The first, and most obvious, is that the Internet has forever changed the way we communicate, collaborate, and do business. This starts with the physical network, but is mostly about new channels and devices and ways of connecting—the inventions the network has made possible.

- **Companies are changing.** Companies and cultures are reacting to this flatter, more connected world. There are more global teams, more global products. Even small companies are less likely to be exclusively local, especially for digital products, which can be accessed anywhere. We are changing as individuals, too.
- **We are more connected.** We are more mobile, more connected, and more aware of people outside our immediate environment. We are more likely to live in different places during our lives, and to work with people from many different places.
- **Innovation happens everywhere.** Perhaps one of the more subtle trends is that innovation can come from anywhere. New ideas, and the power to spread them, are not confined to corporate headquarters any more. New forms of innovation have emerged, and the network makes open, distributed collaboration possible.
- **Thinking globally is also thinking locally.** They may seem like opposites, but global and local thinking go hand in hand. Global thinking reaches across cultures to find similarities. Local thinking digs deeply into each culture to understand it and be able to design for it.

The World Is Smaller ... and Larger

Thomas Friedman, the New York Times columnist and best-selling author, wrote in his 2005 book of the same name that "the world is flat." He means that we live in a world in which ideas and work can move freely from one place to another, where anyone can compete in a global market, where the playing field is level—flattened—to give everyone a chance. This wasn't an overnight change. He argues that we are in a new phase of globalization—Globalization 3.0—starting from about the year 2000, which is unique in the way it allows individuals to contribute and compete, no matter where they are from.

Change is never easy. In the short term, there are always dislocations along with progress. Think of the Luddites, weavers protesting new automated looms that threatened their craft and livelihood. But that new technology was one step in creating inexpensive, mass-produced clothing. So some of the opportunities we see for UX may be a loss to some people. Standing on the shores of California, globalization may look like a giant wave of jobs leaving the coast. But, looked at from China or India, Brazil or Africa, this looks like opportunities being created in your own neighborhood.

Everywhere we look, we see institutions that appear the same as they used to be from the outside, and carry the same names, but inside have become quite different. We continue to talk of the nation, the family, work, tradition, nature, as if they were all the same as in the past. They are not. The outer shell remains, but inside all is different—and this is happening not only in the US, Britain, or France, but almost everywhere.

Anthony Giddens - The Runaway World (1999)

Population Matters

Pick up any article on world business, and you'll see business statistics that make it clear just how important the "emerging markets" are. All you need to do is look at any map of the world population. There are a lot of people in China, India, and the rest

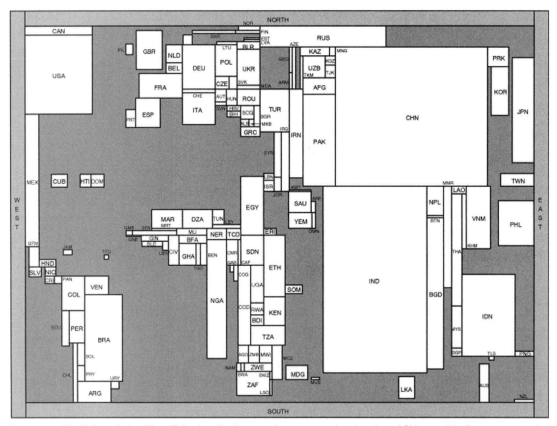

Figure 2.1 World Population Map. This visualization puts into perspective the size of China and India as compared to the rest of the world. Each country appears as a rectangle proportional to the size of its population. http://www.win.tue.nl/~speckman/Cartograms/WorldCarto.html.

of Asia. That's a big market, as the business and marketing press tells us nearly every day. All those people are changing the global commerce.

The Internet Is Flat

We all know that US corporate giants like IBM, Google, Yahoo!, and Apple are global, but we can also look to examples like Infosys, Philips, Samsung, and Lenovo. One of the consequences of a flat world and the connections the Web makes possible is that even small companies are now global. Person-to-person travel sites (like airbnb.com) rely on being international to create a critical mass for their products. Sites like ETSY (etsy.com) let people who make handcrafts from around the world reach audiences anywhere. Someone in the United States can order a piece of jewelry from a craftsperson in Israel and ship it to a friend in New Zealand.

Sometimes the flatness of the network means that products find a market they weren't looking for. One example of this is Igniter, a dating web site with a unique twist: first dates are in a group of people. About a year after the site launched, the company noticed that there was a lot of traffic from Asia, especially India, where they were adding hundreds of users a day in the bigger cities. Soon, they decided that they were really an Indian dating site: 80 percent of their users live in India. They began to grapple with both cultural references and practicalities about payments and the popular mobile devices. Now, they have decided that they can't run an Indian business from New York, and are setting up an office in India where each partner will spend several months each year. They didn't plan to start a global business: customers came and found them from an unexpected part of the world. Why? Because the site's twist on dating fits into the social culture in India (Markovitz 2011; Seligson 2011).

There are still local flavors to the Web. There are sites focused on local services, written in local languages. And there are local favorites: Facebook may seem global, but in Brazil most people are on Orkut; in Japan, it's Mixi. Is this a considered preference, or simply that those products attracted a critical mass first? It's more useful to be on a social network with your friends. When interaction designer Calvin Chan arrived in Japan from Canada, "I would say to my new friends, do you have a Facebook account, and they would just say, what...? They don't even know what Facebook is. Because they have Mixi, they have their cell phone e-mail address. They have their own ways to connect."

Companies Are Changing

Creating global products seems to come in stages, starting with simple translations and basic internationalization, then thinking about cultural differences, and finally working toward a deeper understanding of people in different places. "The challenge for moving forward," Michele Visciòla said about his company's work with many different large corporations, is to be able to "embed other cultures into your own culture." Companies that can't do that can have trouble rising above their local biases and assumptions. Unfortunately, for all the stories we heard about doing research in many markets, some people said that they are still trying to convince their companies and even their research teams that they need to be thinking internationally.

Being Global

The basics of making a product that can be localized are not new or even particularly difficult. Like usability or accessibility, it's better when they are built in from the start. It's perhaps surprising to hear in 2011 that any digital product isn't automatically built to be ready for internationalization. In many cases, these are simply the practical considerations of things like currency and date formats—things that are just a matter of good "hygiene."

Some companies however, include globalization in their product design strategy. Trend Micro, where Hsin Eu is director of a global team creating the user interface for security products is one of them.

> Thinking about deep customization early makes it easier for the technical builds to be flexible enough to accommodate customization. We often decide what functional modules to include, or even swap out modules for specific markets. This might be presentation and brand, like the visual design and style or the product spokesperson, but even behaviors can be customized. For example, a summary page with a lot of alerts might be appropriate in North America, but would seem too aggressive in Japan. Both the technical module and the behavior need to be flexible.
>
> **Hsin Eu**

Being ready starts with market knowledge, to be ready to react to opportunities in local markets. The people who described the strongest global strategies at their company also talked about doing constant research and watching market information.

When your products and initiatives cross borders, you can't be successful unless you have a good understanding of those markets.

To create experiences that work for many places and cultures, companies and their UX teams have to recognize underlying similarities as well as differences, whether this is similarities in the structure of a task or human truths that relate to their own product.

When you sell products around the world, you might have a single marketing campaign used everywhere, but you are more likely to tailor the way you present the message to speak to local markets. A regional director for an advertising agency with offices around the world, Mark Webster talked about how they find an underlying universal message for laundry detergents.

> We've created a message about letting little Johnny or Mai Wei go off and play, explore, and get dirty. It's natural, it's what kids do. And, it's giving mothers 'permission' to let it happen because we have a product that will make his clothes sparkling white when you wash them. We're tapping into a universal truth that mums don't like to see their kids get dirty. But, instead of being angry with them, we want them to trust the brand's vision and see the good side to dirt. Whether you're talking to a mother in rural Vietnam or urban Guangzhou, it's the same motivation. They want their kids to play and have fun, but then they want to proudly see them go to school in a bright, white shirt.
>
> **Mark Webster**

Changing Relationships

Companies often start out geocentric, with strong cultural ties to their home country and decisions made from headquarters, whether that's the United States, Finland, or India. But globalization forces them to rethink that focus.

We talked to one IT service company that started as a very local Indian company. As they started growing, they had to figure out the relationship between their regional offices and their headquarters. Their strategy has been to hire locally, so that they have people who know the local markets in distant places like Europe and the United States.

We heard about a lot of approaches to organizing companies:

- Fully global teams, with team members in many countries and no single center except the place where the leader of a team or project happens to be
- Central UX teams that set standards and develop templates as a way of creating a strong design approach even though product design teams might be located around the world

- Central teams that support local affiliates that are largely independent; in some cases, the local product really comes from a separate operating company, sharing a global brand.

Each of these approaches has its advantages and challenges for managing the user experience of global products.

Developing Local Talent

A common theme that we heard from people managing design teams is the need to develop local skills. Some of these stories were about training new talent in markets where the whole idea of UX is still new. Some of this education happens within companies as they expand, for example adding UX to the training for developers. But there are also new design schools springing up around the world. In Pune, India alone, there are now four different programs for architecture, animation and product design, and internationally recognized programs forging new directions in design.

Multidirectional Influences

As local talent develops, innovation and influence flow in many directions. Innovation and influence no longer flow only from West to East or from industrial to emerging countries. This first happens within a country.

For example, the first automobiles to come to India were Western designs imported without change. But those cars didn't work well in the Indian cultural and economic context. With local talent, the Nano cars, developed by Tata, took the basics of a car and transformed the design into something uniquely Indian. Now, the design thinking developed locally has started to flow outward, back to the places that earlier had been the source of all design. Professor M. P. Ranjan, design thinker, author of the blog Design for India, and a former faculty member at the Indian National Institute of Design, is influencing thinking about design and development around the world through his writings, his blog Design for India (http://design-for-india.blogspot.com), and his presentations at the conference of world leaders in Davos, Switzerland.

Appreciating Local Talent

Although we heard about good progress from many of our interviewees, we also heard a lot of frustration from people "in the regions" about not being able to participate as equals.

Necessity Is the Mother of Invention

When companies in India needed more skilled workers than the design and technical schools could supply, they developed innovative practices for workforce development that have helped industries in India compete globally. One study suggests that the United States and other countries facing increased global competition would do well to learn from them. (Wadhwa, de Vitton, Gereffi 2008)

In the past, we had the HQ and the regional, and the HQ had the authority to make all the decisions. I think that situation will change. When real globalization comes, and the information flow becomes faster, each region will be equal and will work equally. That means that each region will find their strength, and we will have to respect each region's perspective. That doesn't mean, I will only take my own local perspective … we should all take a global perspective. Local means the place I live with and the place I work with, and that becomes part of the contribution I can make.

Yu-Hsiu Li

We all want to be respected as an equal, with something important to bring to a project. In his career managing marketing agency offices around Asia, Mark Webster says that it's just human nature. Even people who are working for a global company are still "working with a local client in their own local market. It's human nature to resent things that come from the center office, or to dislike things that are forced on them." It's also human nature to think, "we're different."

New Relationships in Asia

One other trend we heard about from people working in both India and China is the development of stronger relationships among Asian companies and countries. Several people mentioned that Bollywood movies are now including China in their international stories, rather than focusing on Europe and the United States. For example, perhaps a character goes back to China to get in touch with his roots. In the past, this plot would have revolved around "Indian goes to United States, to cowboy-land" not "Indian goes to China."

Anjali Kelkar predicted that this is going to bring a big change. "Right now, something gets designed in India, manufactured in China, and sold to America. It's almost like a linear process. But what will be interesting is when India and China both design to sell to each other's consumer. So far, we have largely focused on thinking about East–West, but East–East will be the next global."

MEASURING THE SHIFT

The Deloitte Center for the Edge has attempted to measure the forces of long-term change in The Shift Index (Hagel III, Brown, Kula-soonriya, Ebert 2010). Part of that work, the Flow Index, measures the changes in social and working practices that are emerging in response to the new digital infrastructure. They see *flows of knowledge* amplified and enriched as people's passion for their profession increases and technological capabilities for collaboration improve. Some of the trends they see are relevant to global UX work:

- People are finding new ways to reach beyond the four walls of the organization for collaboration and inspiration.
- More diverse communication options are significantly increasing the scalability of connections.
- The recent burst of social media activity has enabled richer and more scalable ways to connect with people and build sustaining relationships.
- The rapid growth of Internet activity creates richer opportunities for connection with a wider range of people and resources.
- Virtual connections may not be enough—people increasingly seek rich and serendipitous face-to-face encounters through travel and relocation.
- Workers who are passionate about their jobs are more likely to participate in *knowledge flows* and generate value for companies.
- Investment around the world makes it possible for companies to access global innovations.

In the full report, Measuring the forces of long term change: The 2010 Shift Index, you can see the data behind these conclusions. (http://tinyurl.com/2aon8jl)

We Are More Connected

It's always been possible to collaborate over time and distance—early scientists in the United Kingdom's Royal Society shared advances by postal mail. But it's hard to imagine the kind of fast-paced work of modern product development without the Internet. When Whitney worked on her first project with a distributed team, collaborating between locations in New Jersey and Idaho, "we had phone, fax, and a dial-up bulletin board. No e-mail. No screen sharing. We'd send sketches of a design by fax. Meetings were punctuated by someone running out to the one computer with a modem to retrieve new files from the BBS and carry them back to the conference room on a floppy disk. That was 1990."

It's hard to imagine writing this book without all the bits of technology. With Whitney based in the United States and Daniel in Hong Kong, we had only a few opportunities to meet in person, including two intense workshops, but most of the collaboration was by e-mail, voice and text chat, and sending files around. It's not that it couldn't have been done in the past, but now people can connect so much more easily across continents.

Our work on this book is an example of the sort of casual global collaboration we see on the rise. We conducted most of the interviews across 16 time zones using Skype, arranged by e-mail or instant message. Transcriptions were done by a woman who splits her time between the west coast of the United States and France. We paid her using a Web service. We collected our files online and shared photographs on Flickr. We used search, Google Alerts, RSS feeds, and Twitter to find articles on UX web sites, traditional news sites, and personal blog. There wasn't a single "killer app"—no one technology was critical. What's interesting is how strongly all these tools are woven through our lives and work.

THE NETWORK SOCIETY

Sociologist Manuel Castells sees the rise of the network as the basis for fundamental change in society (Castells 1996). "The speed and shape of structural transformations in our society, ushering in a new form of social organization, come from the widespread introduction of information networks as the predominant organizational form." Networks are social structures that by definition have no center, from which everything is controlled. Instead, each node in a network increases its influence by absorbing more information and processing it more efficiently.

Just as the industrial revolution gave us technologies for the mass production of products, the information age is based on new technologies for communication. They create a new economy that is informational, global, and networked, and make possible global activities "on a planetary scale in real time."

He calls the network the "space of flows" because of the way information moves within it. The network blurs boundaries, making it possible to work within a company, between units within a company, or between companies.

Manuel Castells' primary work, The Rise of the Network Society (1996) is a lot to read, but you can find several of his lectures on You Tube. A good place to start is with this interview: http://www.youtube.com/watch?v=0GBB7U5mv0w

UX and the Network

It's hard to imagine the UX field growing as quickly and coherently as it has without the connection of the network. IxDA, the Interaction Design Association, is an example of an organization without a single center, with leaders and members from around the world. Instead of a community built only around an annual conference, e-mail and social media discussions go on all the time. This allows practitioners in (say) Brazil to compare their approaches and principles to those everywhere else. And to take a more nuanced view to see that even within a country, there are variations in how developed UX practice is. Andy Budd talked about how meet-ups and local conferences have helped create a vibrant community in Brighton, UK.

All this virtual connectivity doesn't mean we don't travel. Meeting face-to-face is still an important part of establishing a working relationship. But it's no longer possible to plan only for teams located in a single place. This means rethinking recommendations that everyone on a team go into the field to do user research together and then stay together for the analysis. When your team has people on three or four continents, as many we talked to do, you have to come up with new ways of staying connected. As Itamar Medeiros, User Experience Manager for AutoDesk, Inc. in China said, "We have to be a lot more disciplined about how we share insights from our interviews. We work within a shared framework of processes and practices. We try to use the same protocols at every location, so the collection of data is structured in a way that makes it easy to feed the data back to a central database that everyone can use. We have interpretation sessions to share the data."

Global Connections and Local Connections

It's easy to get enthusiastic about how easy it is to connect. But we might also remember that change is not always universally positive. All this ability to be part of a global community will have an effect on our local communities. Two voices reflect these concerns. One is from a 10-year-old lecture by an internationally known British sociologist. The other is from the personal blog of a marketing and social media expert.

> Instantaneous electronic communication isn't just a way in which news or information is conveyed more quickly. Its existence alters the very texture of our lives, rich and poor alike. When the image of Nelson Mandela maybe is more familiar to us than the face of our next door neighbor, something has changed in the nature of our everyday experience.
> **Anthony Giddens - The Runaway World (2009)**

> There's little doubt that the arrival of the Internet and social media/social networks have increased our global consciousness (and probably global conscience). I'm just wondering, however, what impact this will have on local consciousness. With the decline of newspapers and diminishing importance of the local TV news, I wonder if we will be more connected to people on the other side of the world, than people in our own communities?
> **Jeremy Epstein - Global vs. Local Consciousness (2010)**

In addition, social networks can also create boundaries that make people less tolerant of others. It may be easier to connect to other cultures on the Web, but access is not enough. We don't lose the cultures we grew up with just because we find others. And these easy connections also make it easy for people to reduce the diversity of their environment by connecting only to people similar to themselves. By making customs and habits more entrenched, this makes designing for a diverse audience more difficult. It can also affect us as designers: if *everyone we know* uses one social network, it can be harder to imagine what it's like to use others (or not to use any at all).

We Are More Mobile

Just as global work used to be exotic, global travel and meeting people from other places was once romantic. It's still exciting to get to meet people from other cultures, but as the world's population has become more mobile, it's less unusual to go to school or work in a multicultural environment. This is certainly true in all of many high-tech centers, where companies often have people from many different countries, especially China, India, and Russia. Robert Barlow-Busch, a UX designer based in Canada, described working in an office in Brussels with 40 people from 17 different countries. It's not surprising to see this sort of mix, when so many people now live outside of their native country at some times in their life. The estimates of the Indian diaspora—people of Indian origin who do not live in India—is over 30 million people.

Major cities have always been very global, with a mix of people from many countries and cultures. Living in one of these areas is not the same as the rest of the country, however, as Bas Raijmakers and Geke van Dijk, who run the creative research consultancy STBY, found out when they moved from the Netherlands to the United Kingdom. "There's a wonderful ethnic mix of people living here and everybody understands this is what London is all about. The UK outside London took a bit longer to get familiar with, and it's still perhaps a bit more foreign to us than London itself."

Universities have also become global, as they attract people from all over the world. To take one example, at the HCII program at Carnegie Mellon University, approximately 40 percent of the students are from outside the United States.

Our HCII students come from everywhere from Canada to Portugal, Brazil—Africa is represented this year. We've had folks from Sweden, Middle East, from Jordan and Iran. We had our first Iranian student last year and another young man is coming this year. We also at times represent Germany, Italy, France, Korea, China, Taiwan, Vietnam, Japan, and various countries all over. We have had folks from Greece and Turkey and India. Now, we are getting more applications from Asia—China, Korea, Taiwan, and India.

Jenna Date

A world like the one Anne Kaikkonen encountered when she worked with a person "from one very small town in the countryside of Finland," hardly exists any more. "This person's family, as long as he can remember, for hundreds of years, they have been living in this one particular place or village." She contrasts this with her daughter's generation, who "are more flexible and more open in moving around, thinking more globally, more widely. They don't seem to be kind of as attached to one particular location as much as maybe the generations earlier."

Building Connections

Travel can build connections. Some of our interviewees found that opportunities to travel create a greater sense of curiosity about other places and understanding other cultures. Others started with an interest in another culture, and looked for opportunities to travel and work there. And many of the people we talked to had early travel experience. Their families moved, or simply traveled a lot, so they had a chance to experience many different cultures while they were growing up.

I was very fortunate as a child, my parents took us to travel all across the Indian subcontinent. Even though we are of that heritage, actually being in south Asia, traveling across south Asia, interacting with people and seeing how people live—at the time I probably didn't appreciate it as much as I do now—but I definitely think that made a huge impact on how I view the world.

Kaleem Khan

Perhaps thinking globally starts by simply experiencing more of the world. Janna DeVylder grew up in the US Midwest, but now lives in Australia where she is a principal at Meld Consulting. She didn't expect it to be very different, but finds herself noticing cultural issues more, because she can see them as an outsider. "At the end of the day, my children's lives will be so much broader and more enriched. It will just be a way of life for them to experience difference and sameness." They will experience the everyday immersion of "going to the grocery store and buying food and letting go of the fact that the chocolate just tastes different."

Being a Global Person

A lot of the people we interviewed had done extensive travel. This is not surprising, given our focus on global work. But there were some whose travel and work experience were more local. Despite this, they often seemed no less "global"—just people with fewer stamps in their passports. You can think of yourself as a global person, even if you haven't traveled a lot.

In one interview, Daniel spoke with Peter Grierson in Australia. Together they wondered whether we are seeing a self-selection. Maybe the ability to interact with other cultures, whether through travel or virtually, is one of the things that attracts people to UX work. The strong network of professional connections, combined with the sense of personal curiosity that is important for understanding users, creates a sort of "self-generating outward interest" and a focus on designing for many different kinds of people.

> I think of myself as a global person. Before I moved out of Hong Kong, I saw a lot of things from a Hong Kong-ese perspective. Now, with traveling, I get to see different perspectives on both day-to-day and bigger things. I don't want to limit myself to one point of view. I have a strong desire to understand many cultures.
>
> **Calvin Chan**

Innovation Happens Everywhere

A strong theme in both the interviews and the business press is a change in how and where innovation happens. After years of working on outsourcing projects with little scope for doing more than following orders, Jhumkee Iyengar noticed a trend of seeing a broader range of work available in India—adding design and other opportunities to lead a project. Step back, and this seems inevitable.

> Sometimes I think the people from the US think they are the experts. But development in Asia moves very fast. People here understand the concepts, but the problem is that they lack local experience, and have no time to try out their ideas. So maybe short term, knowledge-wise or methodology-wise we may be not as good as the people in the US, but we will catch up very soon.
>
> **Yu-Hsui Li**

UX managers with teams around the world also talked about this trend, and how they are reacting to it. One financial services company, for example, had equal-sized development groups in the United States and India, but a (multinational) UX team based in the United States. When a few people in India expressed an interest in design, a mentoring program allowed them to be part of UX projects, with an increasing level of independence. When programs like that reach a tipping point, the balance of innovation can shift. Jim Neiters, a Senior Director of User Experience for Yahoo! told us that he now finds that the most innovative ideas come from the team in Bangalore, outperforming the one in Silicon Valley.

INNOVATION HEAT MAP

McKinsey Digital took an empirical look at what makes a region innovative. Their data included economic variable along with output like journal publications and patent applications (Andonian, Loos, Pires 2009).

Mapping innovation clusters

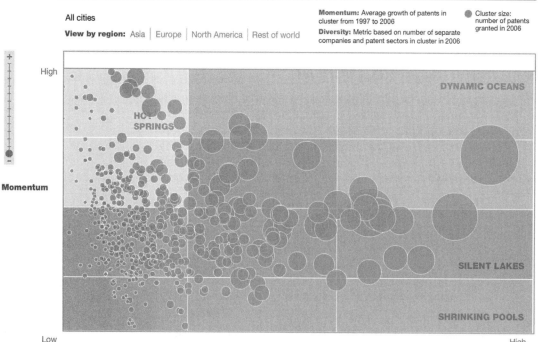

Figure 2.2

They concluded that to support innovation, a city or region must have:

- Basic physical infrastructure and stable governance
- A culture that supports and encourages change
- The ability to attract, develop, and retain a pool of world-class talent
- Diverse companies and industries

It's not surprising to see large clusters of innovation in places like Silicon Valley. But you might be surprised to see that 18 cities with growth rates over 20 percent are all in Asia, India, and Australia.

You can explore their data online in an interactive map of innovation clusters (http:// whatmatters.mckinseydigital.com/innovation/building-an-innovation-nation).

National Innovation Projects

This isn't just a phenomenon in UX. There are projects in many countries to support and encourage innovation. A quick search turns up national projects around the world. Some of these are aimed at accelerating the pace of skills and projects:

- China has an ambitious plan to increase the number of patents, and is likely to lead the world in filing new patents by the end of 2011.
- India is working to close a gap in the number of skilled designers available for projects by improving both the number and quality of academic programs.

Others, especially in smaller countries, are focused on innovation through design as they help their local companies stay competitive in a global market.

- In New Zealand, Better by Design (www.betterbydesign.org.nz) helps companies "increase their international competitiveness by integrating design principles right across their business."
- Finland has launched an "innovation university" to support collaborations of technology, design, and business.

> "Finland is a small nation trying to survive in a global world. We're realizing that design is a key national asset." Professor Korvenmaa, University of Art and Design, Helsinki (Cervi 2008)

UX Growth

All this support for innovation also results in more UX professionals. A 2006 article in Interactions looked at the number of usability professionals in India and China, concluding that both were showing rapid growth. As an example, The Usability Professionals' Association chapter UPA China grew from just a few usability professionals when it was founded in 2005 to over 700 in 2010. Formal and informal groups for interaction design, information architecture, and other UX disciples have also seen explosive growth around the world.

Figure 2.3 Global Usability Labs. The Global Usability Knowledge Management at Florida State University (Douglas 2009) has mapped usability labs in academia, business, and government or nonprofit organizations since 2007 as a way of examining the spread of usability expertise (450 as of this writing). With a focus on physical labs, it does not include organizations that only do ethnographic studies, don't have their own lab space, or use online usability tools. Even with that limitation, this project shows the global spread and growth of usability and UX. http://gukm.lsi.fsu.edu.

New Ways of Innovating in New Markets

With the rise of participation in UX and design strategy, it would be foolish to think that all innovation will follow the same model. As one example among many, in 2004, C. K. Prahalad published *The Fortune at the Bottom of the Pyramid: Eradicating Poverty Through Profits*, one of a number of initiatives rethinking how products are made and marketed for people at the bottom of the social and economic pyramid. Prahalad suggested that by understanding this environment a company could provide social value while also making money in these markets. That same year, Patrick Whitney and Anjali Kelkar described their collaborations between design students at the Institute of Design, IIT and organizations in India.

We are ... focusing specifically on wealth creation in urban slums in the developing world. The goal is to make the local economies more sustainable, encourage the growth of small businesses, and in the long term to help transition residents toward improved living conditions. At all phases, our approach is to develop solutions that harness the entrepreneurial spirit of local citizens.

Patrick Whitney and Anjali Kelkar
Designing for the Base of the Pyramid (2004)

Jugaad
A Hindi buzzword that refers to a quickly improvised, innovative solution. It often points to creativity to make something out of existing resources or by repurposing materials, making do with what is at hand.

This sort of design, focused on social innovation, has been called "frugal innovation." According to Devita Saraf (2009), in an article in the *Wall Street Journal*, it is "innovation that relies more on ingenuity in product, process and people to solve a customer's problem by creative improvisation rather than scientific and technological breakthroughs." In its emphasis on reaching more customers, "It generally starts with serving customers at the base of the pyramid by making the lives of millions of everyday individuals easier" (Saraf 2009).

New Models for Open Innovation

Another innovative concept for innovation is the open network. Loosely defined, these networks pose a problem and invite everyone to contribute ideas or solutions. These projects often focus on social problems that can be solved with innovative design. Some are nonprofit, some run by governments, others by partnerships that can include corporations, academics, and citizens.

- OpenIDEO (http://www.openideo.com) is a process for developing new ideas that allows people to "design better, together for social good." Design challenges are posted on the site, inviting contributions "from inspirational observations and photos, sketches of ideas, to business models and snippets of code."
- As he prepared to take office as President of the United States, Barack Obama's team opened a site that invited citizens to suggest problems for the national agenda and vote on their priority. That sort of open conversation with citizens has continued in the work of the Consumer Financial Protection Bureau to develop new standard financial documents (http://www.consumerfinance.gov/knowbeforeyouowe/) and in other online dialogs with citizens.
- Toyota's Ideas for Good (http://www.toyota.com/ideas-for-good/) was a competition that challenged people to suggest ideas for how technologies created for automobiles could be put to work in other ways.

- Nokia's Open Studios is a process that invites a general audience to workshops to tell their own stories around a design topic in a way that reflects their own needs and those of their community (Rhiain 2010).
- USID Gurukul (http://www.usidfoundation.org/usid) focuses on identifying and solving social and community oriented problems through a collaborative and immersive design workshop. It starts with a virtual Gurukul to prepare participants for the in-person Gurukul workshop, bridging online and in-person styles of working.

Thinking Globally Is also Thinking Locally

We have opportunities today to work with and for people from many parts of the world. More than ever, the saying that we are not our users is an important axiom. The challenges are in how we think about the world, and how we adjust our UX practice to ensure that we consider perspectives other than our own.

Thinking Globally

We asked everyone we spoke with what it means to think globally. All of their answers were about allowing your thinking to cross all kinds of borders—national, cultural, personal. To think globally means reaching across cultures.

> To think globally is to just have a sensitivity to the local cultures and how that might change the standard way that you might design or do research.
>
> **Chris Rourke**

> It's about distance from my own viewpoint. When I'm working further from my own culture, I have to be more vigilant about the kinds of assumptions that I make.
>
> **Josh Seiden**

> Designing globally is understanding the different ways of thinking. So I think global design is to be able to understand and also open the differences or finding ways to gather the knowledge of that.
>
> **Vicky Teinaki**

> To me, it's the people. I can't say Australians are like this, or people in the US like that. What I can say is this: for the user of our product, this is what works for them.
>
> **Tomer Sharon**

It should mean thinking about everyone who is involved. All the different cultures and situations and people who will use the product. On a broader level, "think globally" is about responsibility on a personal, ecological level. Ultimately, both answers come down to awareness and respect. We're no longer isolated companies—we have contact in new ways.

Darci Dutcher

Thinking Locally

They also said that one way to think globally is to think locally. For UX that means the normal work of addressing the needs of the immediate users and digging deeply to understand their culture. In this context, thinking locally could mean:

- Starting from the assumptions and solutions of our own roots, but then looking further to other ways to do things
- Understanding one local geography and then how it compares to other places
- Understanding one market well, so the product fits into the local culture
- Allowing specific local characteristics and circumstances to inform a design for many local places

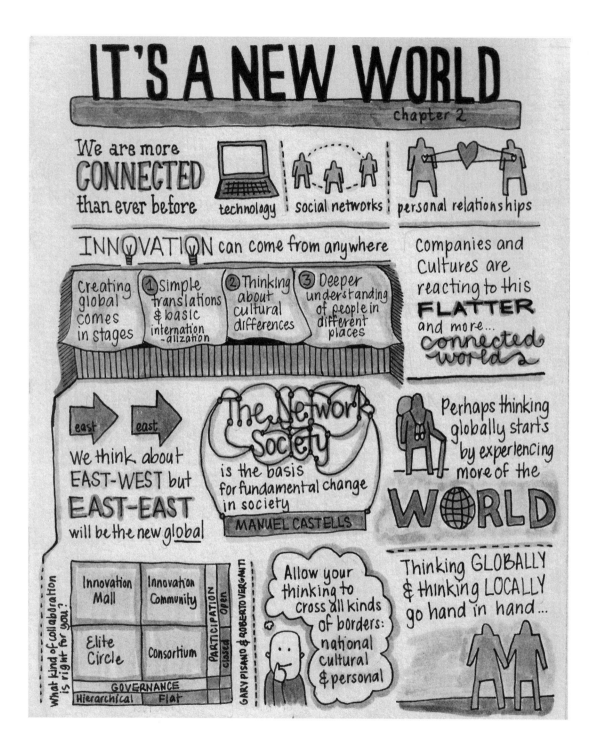

CULTURE AND UX

IN THIS CHAPTER

On my first trip to India, I landed in Mumbai and got on the airport bus. I was soon disconcerted to notice that the driver was busily disassembling the motor. "Excuse me," I said. "Will the bus leave on time?" And was told, "Oh yes, sir." About 90 minutes later, we finally pulled out of the airport.

How many cross-cultural slips and gaps does that small anecdote hold? Attitudes toward time, expectations about appropriate activities, communication style, just to name a few. Aaron Marcus told us that story to illustrate the sort of cultural differences that cause heartaches, conflicts, and misunderstandings all the time. What is acceptable in one culture can be unthinkable in another.

We talk about "cross-cultural design" or "bridging cultures"— what does that mean for UX? User experience is based on understanding users. And users can now seem more diverse than ever. The UX challenges for this new, connected world are based on its biggest benefit: we are more connected.

This chapter looks at questions about culture and what it means for UX

- What do we need to know about cultures to do good UX?
- Are differences or similarities between cultures more important for UX design?
- Are there models that will help us understand culture and apply it in our UX work?
- How much does language matter in design and other UX work?

Delving into Culture

The word "culture" is used in both formal and casual ways. People talk about cross-cultural communication or design that bridges cultures. When we do so, we are usually focused on differences and the difficulties in understanding people who are different from us in some way, and how this affects how they will experience something we design.

Culture is always relative to our own experience. Just as fish don't think about water—they just swim in it—it is only by thinking about how two cultures are similar or different that we can talk about what is unique about each of them. This is important for UX because we always have the challenge of understanding not only our own culture, but other cultures clearly. In the contrasts between cultures, we can see both the similarities and differences that we must design for.

When we think about culture, we have to look beyond individuals to see the whole ecosystem around them. What are the things and the people who surround them and shape their experiences in ways that are relevant to your product? If you were designing a product for school children, you might also need to consider their classmates, family, teachers, and others in their school. A middle class Indian family might also include domestic help, chauffeurs for various family cars, and several generations of family members, forming a collection of overlapping communities and cultural influences.

Culture We Share

Definitions of culture from anthropologists focus on knowledge, attitudes, and customs shared by a group of people, including:
- **Knowledge**: Their patterns of information and knowledge
- **Language**: How they communicate within the group and with outsiders
- **Beliefs**: The customary beliefs and social norms
- **Attitudes**: Shared attitudes, values, and goals
- **Practices**: Values, conventions, or social practices
- **Customs**: Behavior and habits
- **Learned patterns**: Values and behaviors acquired both intentionally and unintentionally

There is one other important criterion: that a culture is shaped by the people within it. As ethnographic researchers Bas Raijmakers and Geke van Dijk put it, "it's something that's being created and re-created by people all the time—not just by certain people, but by everyone as they shape their own daily life." This means that culture is never finished, static. It is always in flux as people adapt to the changes in the world around them.

A Deep Layer

One important aspect of the definition of culture for UX is that we are talking about the deeper aspects that change more slowly than customs, habits, or fashion. Those deeper layers are part of our core cultural identities, usually acquired through our early experiences.

Stewart Brand, the editor of the Whole Earth Catalog and head of the Long Now Foundation, introduced the concept of pace layering. The idea is that different aspects of human civilization change at different rates. Those in the outer layers move quickly, changing often, while the center layers move much less so.

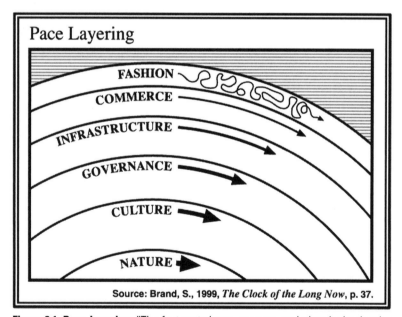

Source: Brand, S., 1999, *The Clock of the Long Now*, p. 37.

Figure 3.1 Pace Layering. "The fast parts learn, propose, and absorb shocks; the slow parts remember, integrate, and constrain. The fast parts get all the attention. The slow parts have all the power." Stewart Brand http://blog.longnow.org/2005/04/11/stewart-brand-cities-and-time/http://longnow.org/seminars/02005/apr/08/cities-and-time/.

Applying this to UX, fashions for social networks or preferences for colors in web site design can change quickly. Patterns in how we communicate or interact with friends, colleagues, and family change more slowly and survive changes in government or commerce.

Nationality and Culture

Nationality—the collection of characteristics we see as similarities among people who grow up in the same country at the same time—is often used as a shorthand way to define cultural identity. There are three problems with using nationality as a shorthand for cultural identity.

First, countries are not a single culture. They are made up of many subcultures, based on region, language, or religion. These subcultures may be very different from each other. This is especially true in large, diverse countries like India, but all countries have subcultures.

Second, in the new, smaller, more mobile, more connected world, values and behaviors cross national boundaries more easily; people and data both travel more widely and more often. Geographical configurations can still matter and affect how easily it is to see new cultures. For example, you might live in some parts of the United States or China and be able to travel for a long way without seeing a substantially different culture, but in Europe, a train ride of just a few hours can cross many borders. Our digital connections, however, can erase distance entirely with instant access and communications.

Third, individuals may be connected to a general national culture, but they are also members of cultures based on their interests, their employer, or the type of technologies they use. Jhumkee Iyengar, a UX design consultant with User In Design in India, summed it up this way.

> "In many ways, India is like a little globe on its own because of all the languages and cultures we have in one country. It's a very old multicultural country, with lots of layers. For a project in India, it would be important to think about differences between rural and urban users. People in my generation in cities have grown up with British and other Western influences. Even on a project for something basic like a banking ATM, I would consider these differences."
>
> **Jhumkee Iyengar**

Technology and Culture

Cultural differences that are particularly relevant in many UX projects may also be based on differences in the adoption of technology. For example, there are generational differences in how people use and think about technologies, depending on whether they are *digital natives*, who grew up after digital technology came into general use, or whether they adopted it as an new way of

Digital Natives
Marc Prensky used the term digital natives in his 2001 work, *Digital Natives, Digital Immigrants,* to describe students who grew up with technology, rather than those who learned to use it as an adult. (Prensky 2001)

doing something. For a simple example, think about what your first phone looked like. Did you have to learn to wrap your head around the idea of using a phone for short text messages?

Companies and Culture

Like any group of people, companies can also develop a culture. That culture can be created intentionally, or grow up as a result of circumstances. Geert Hofstede wrote that every organization has its symbols, heroes, rituals, and values (Hofstede 1994).

- Symbols are words and objects that have particular meaning to the people within the culture. They include the jargon, fashion, and status symbols recognized by the insiders.
- Heroes may be real people—a founder or industry leader—or an ideal, such as the goal for employee behavior.
- Rituals are the group activities. They include celebrations, but also rules of behavior that govern the social norms for the group.
- Values are deeply held beliefs or feelings. They are often unconscious and set the baseline for what is expected or normal.

Professions also have cultures, with shared attitudes, values, and language that connect people in a field. Specialized symbols, heroes, rituals, and values are easy to see in professions like financial services, health care, and other specialized fields, including UX.

In some cases, the basics of the work are the same everywhere in the world, although there can also be local regulations and practices, such as variations in banking practices or insurance regulations. In others, the profession can feel like a whole different world. Working in those fields can be as challenging as working across any cultural divide.

When I was working in financial services, I honestly felt like my users were from a completely different culture. We walk down the streets shoulder to shoulder but we live in parallel universes; the New York financial world and the New York world I grew up in. Traders speak a language all their own. They'll talk about the movement of a stock during the day and they are using English but if you don't know the lingo, you have no idea what they're talking about. It's a very specialized professional dialect. It's not that it's a technical language. It's just the way they talk in slang. They'll say things like the stock is getting hammered right now, and you have to know what that means.

Josh Seiden

For someone designing an application for civil engineers, the biggest challenge is getting to know the details of the technical field. On Itamar Medeiros' team at AutoDesk in Shanghai, "No one on our team has first-hand knowledge of, for example, designing high voltage power lines. When a designer first joins the team, the engineering drawings look like *The Matrix*—just numbers. It makes it even more important that we go into the field and immerse ourselves in their world."

Will Evans, who is currently leading a UX group at a new startup, says that communicating across the different disciplines in the product team can also be a challenge. He's working on ways to create sustained collaboration between developers, product managers, graphic designers and all the rest of the roles. His goal is to create enough cross-cultural learning that anyone can participate in any activity and in creating any artifact in their process.

ZAPPOS COMPANY CULTURE

At Zappos, Tony Hsei set out to build a corporate culture that would support his brand vision. He wrote in his blog, "At Zappos, our belief is that if you get the culture right, most of the other stuff—like great customer service, or building a great long-term brand, or passionate employees and customers—will happen naturally on its own. We believe that your company's culture and your company's brand are really just two sides of the same coin. The brand may lag the culture at first, but eventually it will catch up. Your culture is your brand."

You can read about the Zappos training process and their 10 cultural values at Zappos.com. (Hsei 2009)

UX and Layers of Culture

As important as culture is, some of the issues that UX considers are not, strictly speaking, cultural. UX design has to consider not only the characteristics of users, but also the technical or business environment and the nature of the tasks or interaction. For some products, the task itself may be relatively consistent. For example, in working on hotel-booking web sites around the world, Giles Colborne, from the UK consultancy, cxpartners, found that the basic task is very similar across cultures. "People go through the same fundamental steps. The things that make it different in each country operate on a number of levels. The challenge is the unexpected things that make a difference. Nuances in color and tone of voice turn out to matter a great deal internationally."

One way to organize the issues in global UX work is by how easy or hard it is to predict the issues that users will experience for a specific product. For example, some aspects of a task may be affected by objective facts—the technical infrastructure, legal rules, or competitive products available in a market. Anyone who takes the time to ask the right questions can identify these issues. Language and cultural issues, on the other hand, are more difficult for someone from outside the culture to identify, as they are often based on subtle differences. The implications of this affect the kind of research you need to do, from a simple phone call or web search to contextual user research. It also suggests that you can organize your research efforts so that you can begin with simper methods that collect information that is easier to discover and then build to more extensive immersive research, addressing subtler issues.

At first, we thought this was just good research planning, not particularly relevant to the question of *global UX*. But then we started to notice stories about gaps in understanding basic aspects of the user experience in specific markets. For example, when Jhilmil Jain was in China, leading a team's first user research project there, she noticed that entering text using Chinese characters was "almost impossible" with her company's netbooks. Her good personal experience of using similar products in Hindi (also an alphabetic language) had led her to assume that the design issues in creating keyboards for other scripts were "basically solved" so she was surprised to find out how little they knew about making it easy to use standard keyboards for nonalphabetic languages.

Kevin Brooks, UX Product Manager at Motorola Mobility, also told us about a situation in which unacknowledged cultural issues affected a project. In this case, the cultural gaps were within the team, which had a research and design group in the United States, engineers in India and Italy, and user interface developers in Russia. The problem was that the team didn't recognize how culturally sensitive the product really was. The design group had (unfortunately) done little research, instead relying on their own experiences for the design. This meant that they didn't recognize the extent to which they had expressed their own cultural perspectives, or how different those of developers from other places might be. It also meant that they did not have many detailed stories to share with the UI developers that would explain what they were trying to do. Not surprisingly, the two groups could not agree on what the product could look like. More time understanding their own cultural differences and how they affected the product might have let them work through these issues in the design in advance.

LAYERS OF CULTURE

Thinking about the layers of culture they need to understand for global UX, Giles Colborne and cxpartners see them in a spectrum from easy to predict, to hard to predict.

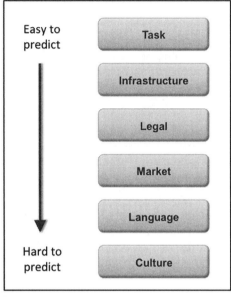

Figure 3.2

Tasks: Booking a hotel, buying a shirt—the users' template of a task is fairly consistent from country to country. Once you know the task in country A, you'll have a good idea how people would like to do it in country B. This is the task outside of the technology.

Infrastructure: The infrastructure can affect users' use of technology. For example, when using the Internet means pay-per-minute, users restrict their access; when broadband speeds are high, users are more tolerant of video and Flash. Statistics on this for different countries are usually available from industry sources and economic monitoring organizations.

Legal: A phone call to your client's office should make you aware of legal issues such as taxes or tax exemptions, privacy laws, or accessibility regulations. These may have a profound effect on task though, such as a need for internal travel visas in Russia that makes hotel booking more complex.

Market: Market norms can change users' expectations of task. For instance in one market it may be the norm for cars to come packaged with lots of features; in another, cars may be basic and the features available as add-ons.

Language: Although translations of words may appear simple, subtleties in meaning can have a profound influence. For example, on the Lexus site, German users expected "technical specifications" to be more "engineering" than UK users who expected "performance and dimensions."

Culture: Everything else. Social attitudes to betting (acceptable or not), role of family, social status of roles, what is considered to be "clean," food rituals, holidays, justice, public and personal morality, society vs. individual, good manners, tone of voice, cultural icons, hopes and fears.

Finding Difference and Sameness

We asked everyone we interviewed about differences and similarities between cultures. A funny thing happened: most people wanted to talk about what was the same, or universal, challenging the notion that "global" automatically implies differences. The fundamental things, they said, don't change, or change slowly.

> The things we value: children, education, the ability to laugh at yourself. Some of these things are very human. That doesn't change because of where you live.
>
> **Jhumkee Iyengar**

> At the end of the day, we all breathe, we all worry about our family. Maybe there are different degrees, but I'm sure that if we did similar research in Thailand or Germany or South Africa, many of the same issues would come up. Some things are just core.
>
> **Janna DeVylder**

That doesn't mean there is not variety around the world. In fact, many people who go into UX *like* the variations and textures of different cultures. People we interviewed described, with some dismay, the degree to which some of the variation seems to be disappearing. When you land in Beijing and the first thing you see is a gigantic Starbucks sign (as Whitney did), or US food chains and even a 1950s style American Diner in South America (as Jim Hudson did), you might start to wonder why you flew all that way. Bill DeRouchey, the UX designer for BankSimple, thinks about both global patterns and local variations.

> If you go to another country, almost the first thing you experience is the airport. And they all fundamentally work in the exact same way. You're just trying to figure out if I'm going left or I'm going right. There's a universal pattern to stuff like that. You're just figuring out the local flavor for how it's accomplished. It starts to change and reveal itself, the further away, of course, you get from immigration. As you go through those doors and then you hit the hall and you get out of the hall and you hit the taxis, and you start to see both elements that are the same and elements that are very different about a taxi experience.
>
> **Bill DeRouchey**

The way people described some projects was like this, especially for relatively straightforward tasks: booking hotel rooms, checking for viruses, e-commerce, ticket kiosks, or banking. They said something like, "It's the task. That doesn't really change from place to place. The basic steps are all the same." At Google, Tomer Sharon found that the similarities of new technologies and businesses built around them were often stronger than regional cultural differences.

> On one project, I thought there would be differences between North American and European customers, because our project managers thought that they were hearing different needs being expressed in Europe. In the end, I don't think it was a deep cultural difference. I'm trying to be very practical. For every study, there is a set of research questions you need to answer. Even if you say, "There is no difference," it's still an answer, so it's not a failure.
>
> **Tomer Sharon**

As we kept talking, however, almost everyone came up with an example of the local flavor and preferences that make a lot of difference in designing a user experience. These examples included some infrastructure basics, like different types of payment methods, regulations that have to be acknowledged and designed for. This is true for products used in daily life, as well as for the high-tech products that Doug Wang designs.

> Normally, when a designer takes a task, we are looking at one problem. But no problem is stand-alone: they connect to other things. Even a single work flow is influenced by what happens upstream and downstream. So to achieve our (design) task, we might have to talk to 20 other people. We are actually looking at the knot in a net.
>
> **Doug Wang**

As people talked through the complexities of a design, each detail hinted at the contextual forces that shaped it. A good example is designing banking apps in the Middle East. There are some simple visual issues, such as designing for a language that is written right to left. But there are also the broader requirements of creating a banking application for the Islamic community that will be acceptable under Sharia laws and consistent with cultural customs of how a family makes important financial decisions. In this case, deep layers like language and religion interact with shallow layers like banking laws and commerce to affect the conversation. It's hard to separate culture from user experience because the two are so intertwined.

Relevant Differences

Maybe we focus on differences because it's easy to assemble lists of things that are different. This is a philosophical debate as much as anything else between anthropologist and practical designer. We are a little bit of both of them. Even the questions we choose to ask—or not ask—are part of our stance. The question is what are the differences that are relevant for UXD in general, or for a particular project.

> One of the things I learned early in my career is be sensitive to the differences that make a difference. I think that in the early days of user centered design, we were really focused on what are the differences between this and that, between this person and that person and this group and this culture and that country and this and that. But it's really important—I think the question we really need to ask ourselves as designers is when are we looking at a difference that makes a difference, and which of these differences at the end of the day don't actually make a difference. That can be sometimes hard to judge.
>
> **Robert Barlow-Busch**

Some examples of differences that might—or might not—matter are:

- The utensils used to eat with or whether a fork is held in the right or left hand
- How taxi drivers calculate the fare for a ride
- How mobile phones are shared in a family
- Preferences for bright or muted color schemes
- Ways of addressing people by name
- What people eat for breakfast
- The most popular social media program
- Typical working hours for office workers

It can be easy to think that countries with a shared language and cultural heritage will have the same user experience, but there may be important differences between otherwise similar countries. In their work for The Open University in the UK, Caroline Jarrett, a UX consultant based in the UK, and Whitney, from the United States, found many differences in their assumptions about higher education, including the structure of a degree program costs, and attitudes about universities. Ronnie Battista, an experience design director, says that the small differences may be the most important.

> Global research often conjures images of multilingual facilitators and discussions of the cultural elements of design based on geography, but in testing an internal application with a large global

utilities company, we found differences between employees in the US and UK. As expected, we uncovered numerous shared issues, but there were smaller ones that we found in language discrepancies. For example, in the US, the word "monitor" was associated with the verb (e.g., to monitor a dashboard), whereas in the UK "monitor" was the actual terminal screen where they entered the information. A small distinction, but when dealing with the global provision of highly flammable gases, it's basic communication issues that can be the most important in critical situations.

Ronnie Battista

Determining what differences, or what aspects of local culture and customs are relevant is especially important when you are looking at many countries, not just one or two. Jim Hudson made the point especially forcefully. He manages research for PayPal in Europe and the Middle East, covering more than 20 countries. He has to decide whether to think about Germany and France as similar (because they are both European countries) or different (because they have their own language and customs). Working for PayPal, he might focus on the most popular payment methods, and look for groups of countries that are similar in this behavior and then for those that are exceptions. In a comparative study of checkout processes between online bookstores in the United States and the United Kingdom, for example, he did not find any significant differences. But if you don't understand how the unique Brazilian payment method, the boleto, works, you will never be successful in e-commerce there. That helps him make decisions about where to put research and design resources to have the most impact.

The Question of Hofstede

Trying to get your head around all the issues in understanding culture begs for a model that can organize all the elements and help you start thinking about how to use cultural information in design.

The model most people reach for is Geert Hofstede's cultural dimensions. It's certainly the most quoted, with some of the dimensions now part of general terminology. Concepts like "power distance" and "collectivism vs. individualism" came up in conversations without any special reference.

If you haven't seen this work before, it's a simple model, with five dimensions upon which any culture can be classified. It's based on quantitative research over many years, starting with a study of IBM employees around the world.

HOFSTEDE'S DIMENSIONS

1. **Power distance,** or the degree of inequality among people that the population of a country considers as normal, looks at how much people accept and expect that power is distributed unequally (from relatively equal to extremely unequal).

2. **Individualism,** or the degree to which people in a country have learned to act as individuals rather than as members of cohesive groups such as extended loyal groups and families (from collectivist to individualist).

3. **Masculinity,** or the degree to which "masculine" values like assertiveness, performance, success, and competition prevail over "feminine" values like the quality of life, maintaining warm personal relationships, service, caring, and solidarity (from tender to tough).

4. **Uncertainty avoidance,** or the degree to which people in a country prefer structured over unstructured situations and their tolerance for uncertainty, ambiguity, and diversity of approach (from relatively flexible to extremely rigid).

5. **Time orientation,** or the degree to which thrift and perseverance, respect for tradition, and fulfilling social expectations are valued (from long term (LTO) to short term (STO)).

Geert Hofstede, Cultural Dimensions, http://www.geert-hofstede.com/ (Hofstede, Hofstede, Minkov 2010; Hofstede 2001).

Just mentioning Hofstede brings out strong reactions. Despite how often Hofstede is mentioned—especially regarding power distance and individualism dimensions—his work is controversial for several reasons:
- Conflation of nationality and culture
- Focus within IBM, already a transnational organization
- Focus on management, not design

For some, Hofstede's dimensions have the value of being a starting point for their own investigations and as a framework on which they can hang their analysis of patterns of behavior. It's useful for researchers like Katharina Reineke, who are looking for ways to manage personalization in a culturally sensitive but automated way. Her work to allow culturally-based personalization started with discovering that her European approaches to e-learning didn't work well in Rwanda. In her research for her Ph.D., she developed an approach that enables user interfaces to automatically adapt their visual presentation and workflows to the preferences of users depending on their cultural background. She used some of the Hofstede dimensions to create a measurable scale that she can turn into an software algorithm. But she also found that she needed personal characteristics like age to be able to predict preference well.

Aaron Marcus tried using the dimensions and thought about how they might affect design. This was in 1993, when the idea was novel (at least in the United States), but in the end, he found it hard to translate these theoretical concepts into design principles. Filip Sapienza also tried to apply Hofstede's broad quantitative model to his own research with bicultural groups of US Latinos and Chinese-Americans. Rather than scores that fell between their two countries, as the model might predict, participants' scores fell outside the ranges for either one. He concluded bicultural populations, especially immigrants, "experience wide shifts in their cultural sensibilities when transitioning from one society to another" (AM+A 2001; Sapienza 2010a, 2010b).

Ultimately, attitudes toward Hofstede (and other ways of looking at culture) may come down to the difference between social scientists and ethnographers—between a top-down quantitative view that offers a strong model and a bottom-up qualitative view that offers rich description. Hofstede's dimensions may be valuable for defining descriptive concepts, even if they are not as useful as specific research in the appropriate context for making design decisions.

Ann Light (2009) writes that Hofstede "is held up as evidence that tidy answers exist somewhere to untidy problems." Her report from an OzCHI 2008 workshop suggest that as important as Hofstede's guidance on cultural diversity is, for design research, if you want to understand a very different culture, you have to get firsthand experience, not design from a recipe book. Her article concludes: "So if you're designing for a culture you're not familiar with, here's the best advice: read Hofstede's work and put it back on the shelf with everyone else's. Then engage in 'good listening' with the people you're designing for. Use cultural guides and technical probes to help bridge the communications gap. And keep your attitude and methodology flexible—the unexpected is where the most important ideas await. Talk to others who do this work and are interested in cultural perspectives."

A FRAMEWORK FOR SOCIAL CHANGE

Models may be more useful for helping UX designers understand cultural influences when they focus on specific types of attitudes or behaviors that are relevant for specific types of projects. When Experientia, an Italian UX company, worked on a social change project in Finland, they developed a framework to help designers understand the different forces that influence whether people will make changes in their attitudes and behaviors.

One of the challenges of designing for social change is that the products cannot simply fit existing contexts, behaviors, or attitudes, because its goal is to change those very things. Instead, they focused on different aspects of motivation. This model allows designers to tailor their program for a specific context in specific ways.

Their model, for example, defines four different kinds of actions that need to take place for social change.

- **Engagement and Awareness**: Ways to present meaningful and contextual information. Engagement with a new behavior is more likely to be sustained long term if it is easier and more convenient than previous patterns; for example, making it easier to recycle technological waste products or creating systems that automatically reuse grey water in gardens without any extra effort.

- **Community Actions**: We are social animals and react to our neighbors' or peers' behavior. Change requires creating a pool of shared knowledge, accessible to all members of the community, and putting support mechanisms and networks in place to encourage compliance.

- **Self-Assessment**: To translate understanding into action, people need to be able to see the real impact of their individual or group actions. Includes immediate feedback and rewards, from emotional satisfaction. At a community level, the ability to evaluate joint consumption and carbon emissions is an important tool for highlighting the need for further action, and the opportunity to reward sustained change.

- **Leading by Example**: Encouraging individuals to change is vital, but the impact has to occur at the community, regional, and national level. This acknowledges the broader context.

You can read more about this work (Vanderbeeken, O'Loughlin, 2010) at http://www. experientia.com/blog/experientiasframework-for-behavioural-change-towards-sustainable-lifestyles/

Language and Culture

To talk about culture, we must also talk about language. What people say, the actual words they use, and what they mean by them is one of the three sources of information (along with the way people act and the artifacts they use) that ethnographers draw on in understanding a culture.

Communication and Context

In a keynote at the UPA 2004 conference, Ginny Redish, the usability, content strategy and plain language thought leader, talked about communities. She pointed out that we all belong to many communities, which are often tied together by how they communicate. Drawing on her training as a linguist, she also noted that we may use different choices of words and styles of speech in each of our communities.

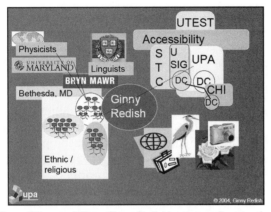

Figure 3.3 Yours, Mine, and Ours. Ginny Redish's community map shows how her different interests and the groups of people she is part of are both separate and overlapping http://redish.net/images/stories/PDF/YoursMineandOurs.pdf. (Redish 2004).

For some, this might mean using different languages. People in India typically speak two or three different languages: one language within their family, the Hindi national language, and English. Each is used in different social contexts. But even if you only speak one language, you probably talk differently to your family, your professional colleagues, and your acquaintances.

We may also want to communicate with different types of companies (and products) in different ways. Facebook might sound more like the way we talk to our friends, but we might prefer our bank to maintain a bit more formality. These preferences reflect both our personal style and cultural trends.

THE TRAP OF THE ANGLOSPHERE

From inside the Anglosphere, as the group of English-speaking countries is called, it's easy to think that everyone speaks English, especially because it's so often the language of international business or lingua franca of tourism. But most of the world speaks something other than English as their *first* language, and 75% speak *no* English at all.

Instead of joining the world together, language can create local clusters of sites—walled gardens—in languages like Chinese, Hindi, Portuguese, or Russian. Ethan Zuckerman, who created GlobalVoices to collect and translate blogs from around the world says that there is not one big global Web. "The Internet has become a bunch of interlinked but linguistically distinct and culturally specific spaces."

(German 2010; Kettle 2010)

Cultures and Communication Styles

Even something as simple as a store clerk saying "Have a nice day" can be a cultural marker. The British might think it's forward of them and injecting personal sentiment into a passing encounter, while Americans simply think it's polite. This intersection of culture, business, and interface interests Noriko Osaka, a UX consultant working on global products from her base in Japan.

When I review international projects, I often recommend changing wording on the interface to avoid being unclear. For example, instead of using "Submit" on the Submit button, in Japan it would better to use "Complete this reservation." Also, we always provide samples of the input for a form to help users, because we have different types of characters in the Japanese language.

I was once told by a British researcher that we enjoy the best service in Japan for free. Let's say you get on the train in Tokyo, and you will hear a lot of announcements by the conductor; for example, on a hot day, you may hear, "We will turn on the air conditioning from now on, as it is getting hot, thank you for being patient in the crowded train." And on a rainy day, they might say, "Be careful not to leave your umbrella. Today we find many of them left in the train." You may think this is too much for an adult, however that's the way it is here.

Noriko Osaka

Both the rules of the grammar and habits of speech add subtle differences of meaning. Languages may require you to name the gender of a person you are talking about, or when an event happened. If you don't understand these differences, you may not really understand what someone is saying to you, or the implications of what you have said.

In the Chinese language, if I want to propose two options, I should put my preferences in the last position. If I say "hamburger or pizza" I'm saying that I want pizza, so that's why people say "yes, let's have pizza." From their perspective, I'm suggesting that they should take the last thing that I'm offering.

Itamar Medeiros

Bridging the gap between two cultures requires understanding how their languages are both the same and different. The debate over the relationship between culture, language, and how we think is summarized in a New York Times Magazine article:

> If different languages influence our minds in different ways, this is not because of what our language allows us to think but rather because of what it habitually obliges us to think about....The habits of mind that our culture has instilled in us from infancy shape our orientation to the world and our emotional responses to the objects we encounter, and their consequences probably go far beyond what has been experimentally demonstrated so far; they may also have a marked impact on our beliefs, values, and ideologies.

Guy Deutscher (2010)

Even if you don't speak the language, learning even a little bit about it can help avoid misunderstandings. When you are getting to know a culture, the slang and jokes can be the hardest to learn, and can easily contribute to communication gaps.

> I think I was on my second day of work and was still getting settled. At the next desk a fellow named Jan, a native Belgian, was on a long conference call with a large team of people, most of whom were in the US. When he finished the call, there were a few moments of silence and then he leaned his head over from behind his monitor with a quizzical expression and said, "Bob, excuse me. Do you have a moment.... Please, tell me what is *crock of shit*?" I guess people on the call had been saying that something they were doing was a crock of shit and he wanted to know exactly what that meant. I spent a lot of time translating English slang and swear words for people. It was great fun.

Robert Barlow-Busch

Nuances of Meaning

Although we can learn to speak a language fluently enough to use it functionally, it is harder to develop the kind of ear for the way language is used that only comes from an insider view. There were many stories about how the meaning of a phrase can differ from one country to another, even if the literal meaning of the words is the same. Sometimes it can be hard to tease out the

> "Never would've predicted the inconsistencies in language b/w American and British English, & how it would impact my effectiveness as a speaker."
> @Whitneyhess, Twitter, May 21, 2010

differences in meaning without the detailed examples that UX research can uncover. Anjali Kelkar's experience as a UX researcher on a project in India shows the danger of making assumptions about the underlying meaning of a word.

For an air freshener product category in China we conducted studies where we asked people to take pictures of their daily life around maintaining their homes. These were followed by in-home interviews with research participants. The marketing team was aware through previous market research that their target audience loved the concept of anything natural. As a result they had recently introduced various 'natural' scented air fresheners such as green tea, tangerine, ginger lily, and so on, but with little or no success in the market.

During the interviews we wanted to probe deeper around whether they could *show* us what natural meant. As we looked at the pictures with one of our participants, I said, "You have a really fantastic house and you are proud of it. Show me how natural is part of it." Finally, she picks up a grainy picture of clothes hanging on the balcony and says, "This one. When there is a little breeze outside, the fragrance of freshly washed clothes blows into my living room, it makes me think there are scented trees outside my home. And that is natural." This was the a-ha moment for my client's team who was present, that *natural* didn't literally mean natural scents, *natural* meant the experience the user had with fragrance in a natural setting. Understanding the nuances of what people meant when they said *natural* was the key to this project

Anjali Kelkar

CULTURE AND UX

chapter 3

Culture is defined by what we share – It is never finished

knowledge | Language | Beliefs | Attitudes | Practices | Customs | Learned Patterns

CULTURE is more than NATIONALITY

Countries are not a single culture

FASHION
COMMERCE
INFRASTRUCTURE
GOVERNANCE
CULTURE
NATURE

PACE LAYERING – Stewart Brand

"The things we value: children, education, the ability to laugh at yourself, some of these things are very human That doesn't change because of where you live" JHUMKEE IYENGAR

DETERMINE YOUR DIFFERENCES

RECIPE BOOK

If you want to understand a culture, go get first hand experience not design from a RECIPE BOOK
– Ann Light –

we may be MORE ALIKE than we think

Hola Hello

You can't talk about culture without also talking about LANGUAGE

Nuances of meaning can be difficult to uncover...

BUILDING YOUR CULTURAL AWARENESS

IN THIS CHAPTER

First day on a new project, and Didi is worried. It's going to be sold in several different countries, but one of the main markets is a culture she doesn't know much about. She doesn't think she can design the experience without understanding the user. Will she do something incredibly stupid? How many stamps do you need in your passport to do global UX?

Designing great global products all starts with the individual. You. How you learn to think about a world beyond your comfort zone and are open to new experiences and new cultures. Thinking globally doesn't mean giving up your identity. As a designer, Steve Baty feels very rooted in Sydney. "That's my home base. I can work with people all around the world, but my perspective is still looking out from that base." But thinking globally is a given today, especially in UX where our work begins with empathy for people. The challenge is to find a way to keep your own perspective while understanding other cultures.

When you start designing outside of your own cultural foundation, you have to really pay attention. If you are not open to those insights, you will miss opportunities to create a deep-seated emotional connection with people. The question is how you take up that personal challenge.

This chapter looks at different ways practitioners have taken on a global perspective and how they face the challenge of meeting and learning to understand new cultures. The themes that emerged around how to build your own cultural awareness include:

- How to learn to "think globally," whether your work takes you around the world or just around the corner

- The importance of giving yourself (and your project) time to get to know the cultures of your audience, immersing yourself in new experiences
- The ways in which building cultural awareness will change your work and your sense of personal identity

Thinking Globally Is a State of Mind

In a presentation at the 2005 UPA conference on designing for global audiences, Jean Luc Doumont ended by saying, "To sharpen your cross-cultural skills, experience more cultures first hand." This is to say that the more different cultures you have met, the more attuned you will be to the nuances of cultural differences and similarities. It does not mean that you can base an entire design *only* on your own experience, no matter how well you may know the culture.

Experiencing new cultures begins with meeting new people, people who may not be just like you. Give it time, and those people may become friends with whom you can share insights to see if they resonate. People you can build a common understanding with, and know that when you talk to them you are on the same page. Colleagues you can just call or send a message to check a detail without long introductions.

Being Open to Others

UX challenges us to look outside of our own experience to find a deep understanding of our users and their goals. Global UX adds the challenge of understanding people whose experience may be quite different from ours.

Almost everyone we talked to used the word *open*. People described themselves as open to new experiences, suggested how important it is to be open to new perspectives, and called *being open* a basic characteristic of a good UX designer or researcher, something they look for when hiring. Building your own cultural awareness starts with extending a basic interest in exploration and discovery to new places and new people. Person after person we talked to said something like this:

> I'm one of those people who love knowing about other cultures
> and new people and different ways of people. I assume not
> everyone feels that excited. They tell me "I go. I get the job done.
> And I come back." But, for me, personally, it's one of the most
> fun parts of life. I guess I just have that natural interest. I love
> talking to people and getting to know them.
>
> **Jhumkee Iyengar**

I'm one of these people that is just an anthropologist by nature. I love people's behavior. I love just watching them. I get a kick out of watching the five different ways that somebody picks up a cup of coffee at a table. I love different cultures and I soak up different cultures and the different mannerisms that come with those different cultures, and the different behaviors and how people are with one another, and the gender roles and the differences between elders and children in that culture. … I'm fascinated on a daily basis by what people do.

Jenna Date

As we read through the interviews, three concepts around being open emerged as a theme:

- **Constantly challenge yourself.** Keep your ears and eyes open and don't give in to the risk of closing your mind off and turning into what Robert Barlow-Busch jokingly called "a curmudgeonly old fart."
- **Exercise your curiosity.** Go into each experience as curious and naïve as possible. Bas Raijmakers and Geke van Dijk echoed many others when they said, "We are interested in people and stories and personal experience, and also in the lives other people are living."
- **Be humble.** Be ready to learn from other people and leave your assumptions behind. Don't assume that your way is the only way or that you know everything. Kevin Lee suggested that, "When you start to be humble about things that you don't know and accept the fact that because you don't know you need to reach out to different people, you start to be really successful."

This may not be easy. You have to be willing and ready to open up to the experience of another culture, rather than just waiting for people from another culture to open up to you. Anjali Kelkar suggests that getting the most out of an experience is partly a matter of attitude. "You have to be calm. Accept that things will go wrong, and then it starts to be fun."

Cross-Cultural Experiences on Every Corner

Perhaps you are thinking something like, "But I wasn't lucky enough to be born into a family where I lived in many different places growing up, and my job doesn't give me the opportunity to travel." It's true that going to new places is an easy way to experience new cultures, but it's not the only way. It's possible to see the world, even if you only go next door. These days we are likely to live near people from other places, especially in larger cities. You may find a cross-cultural moment at a time and place where you least expect it, as Henning Fischer from Adaptive Path did.

> On one of my first research projects, I was doing home visits for a greeting card company. One interview was in Texas, about 45 minutes outside of Dallas. As we arrived, the woman we were there to see came was running across the lawn in high heels, kind of sinking in, with a tray of drinks to welcome us into her house. This was not the kind of greeting I was used to, coming from the upper Midwest. She was very friendly. And very charming, as well. And a very good interview, because she had a lot of good things to say. But at that instant, all I could think was "Life has not prepared me for this moment."
>
> **Henning Fischer**

Kaleem Khan talked about growing up in bilingual Canada, in a neighborhood with many cultures. As part of a minority cultural group, he always had the sense of being a participant observer and has been able to use that feeling in his work. "It is the ability to see multiple perspectives at the same time. I think that's the core of it. But it is also the ability to switch between contexts in a very rapid fashion. As someone who has grown up with those multiple frames, there's a constant evaluation between your personal values and your understanding of the world. This develops a fundamental skill—the ability to remove yourself from your personal frame of reference and see what the world looks like from a different perspective."

Lab, Office, and Tourist Spots

One of the ways to be open to new experiences is to get out of familiar places, like your office, the research lab, and tourist areas. That might be as simple as taking time to wander down a new street or going out of your way to eat somewhere that is not in the tourist guidebooks.

If you take some time out for everyday activities, you might find yourself making connections to your work. When Henning Fischer, from Adaptive Path, went to a Japanese baseball game during a research trip, he wasn't thinking about his project; he was just curious about what it was like to do this familiar thing in a new place. But, to his surprise, "I got an insight that I didn't get through the interviews, even though we were looking at sporting culture. I didn't make the connection until just now. Participating in something that is analogous but not the same helped me understand what I was hearing in the interviews a little better."

Marc Rettig and Kevin Cheng also talked about the value of getting out of "tourist spots" even when they are somewhere on vacation. It's not that sightseeing isn't interesting, but that you don't get a sense of the daily life of a place.

> My first time in Paris, I was traveling alone. I spent a day and went to all the sightseeing places. The Eiffel Tower, the Louvre, Musée d'Orsay. I did it all in a day. The next day it was raining, so I met some people in the hostel. We spent the day in a café, drinking coffee and wine and chatting and watching people go by and watching the garden a little bit. And it felt much more like I had experienced Paris than the day before. The landmark day didn't accomplish much more than to say, "I did it." Other than that, it's really like looking at the postcard.
>
> **Kevin Cheng**

In fact, whenever you visit somewhere new, you can use this technique. It doesn't have to be in a different country. How many of us have seen every part of even one? When Gerry Gaffney worked on a project that took him to schools all around Australia, he got into the habit of taking the train and then walking the 2 to 3 km to his destination. "Walking through the area was a great way to get an idea of what the students experience every day—the shops, the language, some of the social and economic factors. It was much more enlightening than just helicoptering in."

As Aaron Marcus put it, "At Disney's Pavilion of the Nations in the Epcot Center, every place looks the same and smelled the same and all the guides are handsome. Everything was homogenous and artificial. What's important is that you do *something* to achieve an awareness and deep appreciation of how rich and fantastic and wonderful the world is."

Research Maps the Territory

Research is a way of mapping the territory, of making a description of how things are, so that you can create a picture of how things might be. In this conversation we're talking about something deeper than that. We're talking about immersion, which I would say is a way to see the world through other peoples' eyes. You have to be open to the possibility that you might be wrong, and that your experience might not apply because it's from a world that's different.

This isn't just a journey to a different country or a different culture. You can have a cross-cultural experience anywhere down the block. A lot of us go through the world with our attention kind of centered inside ourselves so that we see everything through the boundaries of our own frames. We go to Europe and never get out of our own culture: eat at McDonalds, stay in a hotel, just see some different *stuff*. But you can flip a switch and move your center of attention outside of yourself, and put your history and assumptions and judgments and presuppositions behind. Just see the world for what it is. Like a little kid, you can see everything as new, including you in this place and in relation to this place and these people.

When you actually see through someone's eyes, if you will not just open your mind but open—we'll call it your heart—you might realize that you have been making assumptions all along; that your whole framing of how the world works or what people care about, might be invalid in this situation.

So you need to reframe, create a new description of how the world works and what priorities should be and what people care about. Then you see a better way that might be possible and how that might be organized to create the solution. It's a deeper journey.

Marc Rettig, Fit Associates

Marc credits some of these ideas to Otto Scharmer's Presencing + Theory U, http://www.presencing.com/presencing-theoryu/

A Journey outside of Ourselves

When you are running a user research or usability project, many people told us, the more familiar you are with a culture, the more easily you can interpret what you are seeing and hearing. Your understanding lets you get beyond the surface level of goals and tasks to pick up cultural subtleties, or understand how intertwined an online experience is with daily life. Peter Grierson summed it up well. "The bigger the unknown, the more important the process of immersion is." Finding ways to get to know the culture gives you empathy that will help you not only create a better design, but give you the justification behind the design decision.

Taking Time

Gaining cultural insights takes time, of course. How long, we wondered, does it take to really know someplace? As we expected, we got a range of answers.

Just a few months. Even spending a few weeks or months somewhere changes your relationship to it. That's long enough to start to live an everyday life with regular shopping and the other events of daily life. You learn some of the daily patterns of the place.

> I spent time in Spain and Portugal. One of the biggest examples is just the daily pattern of work. In the US, you wake up, you work all your hours in one big lump and then you go home. In Spain, you wake up, you work pretty much half of your hours of the day, eat a big fat lunch, take a few hours off in the afternoon, then you work the rest of your hours into the evening and then you have a late dinner. Things like that force you to just throw yourself into a situation and figure it out. Just adjust.
>
> **Bill DeRouchey**

Raven Chai, who runs Singapore-based UX Consulting, noticed that when people go there for just a short time, they see it as just another city, like Shanghai or New York. "They bring their own values when they work on projects." But, when they stay in Singapore for 6 months to a year, "they spend time going to nontourist places and begin to understand the language and habits better. They start to fine-tune their mindset when they engage people here. The way they approach their work starts to have a little bit of local flavor. It improves the outputs of the work eventually."

A year at least. People who lived in another country for a year or two talked about going deeper into the culture and seeing their attitudes changing. For some from Western countries, living in another country was a chance to experience life as an outsider. People who moved to a new country talked about seeing their attitudes change when they knew they would be staying somewhere for a long time. Will Evans described the process as "A sense of denial and then a sense of wonder … but clouded by our own cultural prejudices. Sometimes, all we can see is what we want to see."

> I'm living in Japan for a year. In the next 4 months, I think the shock factor will be less and less. I'm already used to the daily life. I don't think I'll see too many more new things. I've seen some change inside myself as well. For the first weeks, I was really annoyed by many of these small customs—the bowing, the interface of the ATM, ticket machine. A very difficult user interface. They have a lot of cute mascots, but they don't make it easy to use. But now, I'm less annoyed by this. Maybe it's because my Japanese reading skills are improving.
>
> **Calvin Chan**

You have to be born there. In the end, you can't ever really know a culture unless you grew up in it. All you can have is a shallower or deeper connection and more or less trustworthy intuition. "Some cultures can take a lifetime to understand," Jhumkee Iyengar told us. "I wouldn't say I know India in all of her complexity, or will know her in this lifetime."

> You will never get to the point where you understand it all. It's possible to understand a great deal, but there will always be part of it that's a mystery. Maybe this is part of the human condition. There are things that the Americans do that just baffle me. There are things that the Germans do that I have no idea about, and have no tie to or understanding, even though I grew up speaking the language. There are many things that I will never understand, and I'm kind of OK with not understanding.
>
> **Henning Fischer**

Martin Polley, who moved to Israel from the United Kingdom, says that he's absorbed the culture of his new country partly through the osmosis of living there and having a local family. Becoming a local means losing the sense that he doesn't look at things the same way as others around him. On the other hand, "there will always be a difference between them and me. For example, I didn't do military service here. They have had that experience, and I never will."

Following Local Customs

No matter how long you have to experience someplace new, you can do it better by setting out to live in the local culture. Calvin Chan suggests that you follow local customs. "Respect how the locals solve their problems. Accept that this is how things are done, even if you don't yet understand the reason for it. They won't tell you these little things, so you must observe quietly and then find the right time to ask questions." Find activities that will let you meet people on their own terms.

> To understand Singapore, try having dinner or lunch with local friends, because people open up over a good meal. Most people here love food, and we like to talk about food … then they tell a lot of themselves. Not in a city restaurant—go to a neighborhood restaurant instead. That's where you will hear the local accent and understand how local people think.
>
> **Raven Chai**

Don't hang out with other expatriates or other people from your own culture. When you can find your own language, newspapers, food, or TV, it can stop you from experiencing the local culture. When Robert Barlow-Busch lived in Belgium, he deliberately decided to live in a town about 25 km outside of Brussels so that he was forced to live in the local community. Anjali Kelkar said that her first years in the United States were easy. "New York City felt multiethnic, like India, so it felt like home. That was partly because I was also able to stay within an Indian expat community there." Her second time in the United States—this time to the more homogeneous Midwest—was more of a shock, as she was forced to embrace US culture more.

Digging a little deeper into the daily life can give you a deeper understanding. Even if you start with an interest in the culture or have exposure from the outside, it's never the same as experiencing it for yourself, by being there.

Living in Japan for three years, Australian Chris Marmo found his understanding of the culture deepen over time.

> Look, people know that Japan is different. It's got a place in pop culture as well, in western society, though—they've actually got a very influential culture in that respect through the animations and things that have come our way and a lot of the kids programming and things like that. So people know about Japan and some of the differences. But it's a shallow understanding. It was the same for me as well. It wasn't until I was in Tokyo and I was spending time in tiny little hole-in-the-wall bars with one of

my Japanese friends, having conversations, telling jokes and things that I really got to understand the Japanese psyche a bit more.

Chris Marmo

Learning the Language (at least a little)

Maren Pyenson, who specializes in globalization projects, prepares for an assignment by studying the language. "It would be irresponsible of me to go to Brazil and expect to able to function without understanding the language." Even if you don't speak the language perfectly, it can help to know enough to follow a conversation. If you are doing usability testing or talking about a product, you have the advantage of something to point at.

Languages also have a style to them. We might say that one language is poetic or another is direct, or talk about how another incorporates the social hierarchy in the differences between casual or formal speech. Chris Marmo found that he adopted a more subdued personality when speaking Japanese. "Making the decision to drop some of the formalities in the language was hard because it was not just a question of the words, but accurately expressing subtle social relationships." If you understand the communication style and social rules, you can make a decision about how to adapt.

For Jennifer Carey, knowing the language made all the difference to her experience of living in two different countries, Italy and Lebanon. "Fluency of language comes with fluency with the culture. You have to work really hard. After two years in Italy, where I spoke the language, I made friends for life. But when we lived in Beirut, we never learned the language because we thought we were only staying six months, and then another and another. There were many other factors—we were working intensely, traveling a lot for work, and there was a larger cultural divide. But even after five years we still don't have the same kind of close friends that we found in Italy."

Finding Cultural Proxies (if you can't travel)

Having said all that, sometimes we simply don't have time for even a quick trip, and have to find ways of learning about a new culture secondhand, through someone who can be your guide. All the alternatives have their limitations, but they are better than doing nothing to build your knowledge and awareness.

The first solution is to find people in your local area who can be your informants. Many of us work in technology companies with colleagues from around the world. Jim Hudson finds people who are experts in an industry by recruiting usability test participants from among people who have just arrived in the company offices from another country.

If you are in a metropolitan area, or can work with participants remotely, you can usually find people with diverse backgrounds for interviews, lab studies, or visits to their own environments. It's not perfect, but Joe Leech calls it a good start at understanding a problem that might get you 20 percent of the way. IEEE, the international engineering organization, makes a point of including participants from around the world in any usability tests.

You also need to be careful of a sort of *time capsule* effect. Immigrant cultures tend to represent the peak period of migration. Very quickly, the community can become quite different than their homeland as people become acculturated in their new country. This is especially important if either country has experienced rapid change. In China, for example, the current generations, who grew up in a more open environment, are quite different from their parents in some ways. Wei Ding, who now lives and works in the United States, finds that on every trip she takes China seems to have changed even more dramatically.

Several people, including Mike Lai, talked about growing up as children of immigrants and how they resisted going to language and culture classes. As a child, he wanted to be part of the local culture where he grew up. Only later, as an adult, did understanding both cultures (and speaking both languages) seem important. Mike now lives in Hong Kong, where he teaches at the Hong Kong Polytechnic University, School of Design.

Even without running a full research project, you can use both local and remote resources and the Web to try to get a sense of a cross-cultural design problem. Kevin Lee uses experts within his organization who have worked in the local market or had more interaction with those customers. "Sometimes designers dismiss those opportunities because they have been trained to talk to users directly," he says, but "sometimes talking to internal folks with long experience working with the same set of customers can give you a view of what works and what doesn't." Customer service staff can be a good resource, because they have listened to a breadth of users. As a UX designer working for a global company, Darci Dutcher can find herself working on a project for users anywhere in the world. She often has to find ways to learn about a new culture in a fast-paced Agile project.

One web site I worked on was in both Arabic and English. This proved to be an interesting challenge for me. I don't read Arabic, so it was hard to tell if just flipping it around to solve the reading direction was good enough. I talked to a lot of people who spoke Arabic and did all sort of web searches to look at Arabic sites for examples. There are quite a few newspapers with English and Arabic versions, so I spent time comparing the two versions to understand how they transformed.

Darci Dutcher

An International Office Brings Cultures Together

I worked at Sony Brussels for two years. Our office had at least 17 different countries represented on a staff of only 40 people. It felt like I didn't have to leave the office in order to travel. Just walking down the hall to grab a coffee, I might hear five different languages.

It was just fascinating to get to know my coworkers, to hear their stories about where they came from, and learn how we see the world differently. I worked closely with a woman who had just relocated from Kiev in the Ukraine. During breaks, she would describe what life was like behind the Iron Curtain and tell these incredible stories about experiencing the fall of Communism. That was fantastic! And eye-opening.

When we needed international insights, I could often simply get feedback from colleagues. There was sort of just a natural flow of information and feedback in the office as we worked together on things. Because our team was so incredibly multicultural, I didn't feel like we had to go very far to get valuable insights.

It helped that our project at Sony was for as highly technical market. My colleagues were, in fact, the kind of people I was designing for. Computers and technology were a common language and a shared culture among everyone there. Our subject matter exerted a pretty strong influence on how people thought about their work and what they expected from tools they would use.

Robert Barlow-Busch

Be Genuine ... and Adapt

When you are open to another culture, two things happen. You learn about it, of course, but it also changes you. And you learn to adapt.

Digging into Understanding

Learning and cultural awareness don't come all at once, and even if you adopt a new culture as your own, you may never feel completely part of it. Both Whitney and Darci Dutcher were surprised at how *different* the United Kingdom could feel for someone from the United States, even after a longer stay or many visits.

> It's layered. When I look back on our seven years in London, I think within the first two years you can feel very at home. I feel comfortable here but that's just a layer. Every year another layer deeper. I feel more grounded. I understand things and smile to myself and realize, I thought I understood things before but I didn't really. That's still going on. We are still outsiders living here. I haven't been growing up here so I miss a lot of things people my age would share who have been growing up in the UK. If you talk about—I don't know—television programs you watched or toys you played with. Often in conversations you notice that you missed that shared history. There are many layers. Tons of layers.
>
> **Geke van Dijk**

Being Human

No matter how well prepared, how culturally aware you are, you are still likely to have at least a few moments when you are (at best) not sure what to do or (at worst) create really cringe-worthy moments. The best advice for those moments is just to be as human as possible.

> The one thing that got us through a situation with a lot of different cultures was our ability to be genuine. Even though people might be doing it consciously, they're reading others in the room. If you're trying to pull off that you know more than you know, people are going to recognize that immediately. Our one trick that's worked in all cultures is to go in and say, "I'm stupid. I'm apologizing now if I overstep my boundaries. If I do something inappropriate, I would appreciate if you would call me on it." We get a much better response if we just say that up front. "We are

not you and we are just trying to understand where you are coming from."

Jenna Date

If you show your readiness to meet people on their own territory and their own cultural terms, they will open up a lot more because they understand that you are approaching them with respect. You can do this through the simple fact of taking time to learn about them, or through how you communicate. As an example, when he was doing requirements work with indigenous people in New Zealand, Peter Grierson went into meetings and interviews "using language that showed that we had some understanding and respect for their organizational structure. Working with the elders in this group was different than working with our typical audience of people in a Western corporation."

Adapting Your Own Behavior

One advantage of living or working in more than one culture is that you grow as a person and professional and can learn to adjust your own style to each environment. You become more adaptable in your behavior and communication style.

> In the US, the way of work is to say to someone's face what is on your mind, and no one thinks twice about it. But in Eastern cultures, you beat around the bush and hope that the person will infer what you mean. When I first worked in the US, I was very shy about speaking up and was very quiet. Then I got used to it. When I came back to India, I didn't like that I had to weigh and think before I spoke. So there was an adjustment in both directions—when I went from East to West, and when I went back from West to East."
>
> **Jhumkee Iyengar**

Sometimes, the adaptation can become a habit. Apala Lahiri Chavan, from Human Factors International, is well known for her work adapting usability methods to local cultures. Talking to Gerry Gaffney on the UXPod podcast (http://www.infodesign .com.au/uxpod), she talked about how an adaptation that worked in England backfired when she returned home to India.

> Now when I lived in England I got completely ... into the habit of saying please and thank you and when I came back it just ... became an involuntary reflex action till I noticed how everybody was aghast at all my pleases and thank yous and I didn't understand what was happening until a couple of my close friends

said to me, "What's wrong with you you've become such a snob, why are you saying please and thank you all the time to us?" and then I realized, Oh My God, I would say the same thing to anybody who came back a close friend or a family member and who started saying please and thank you all the time.

Apala Lahiri Chavan UXPod (2006)

Not all stories end neatly and nicely. Sometimes who we are just clashes with the culture we are trying to work in, no matter how much we try to adapt.

As an American woman working for a Lebanese company in the Middle East, Jennifer Carey definitely had to adapt.

I had to be tougher than I might be in the US. I felt that if I showed any gap in my confidence, there was a risk that I wouldn't be taken seriously. Being American worked to my advantage as a project manager, but I had to work to get men to pay attention. I think I earned my respect by asking good questions. I got further as a woman than I would have expected, but there were limits. As a woman and an outsider, I could run a project, but I couldn't do business. Personal relationships matter here and a lot of them center around socializing in places and ways that, as a woman, it was not possible for me to be a part of.

I made mistakes. I inadvertently ended up humiliating someone on my client's staff by publicly by asking where things were on her tasks in front of the company executives. Asking the question in this way exposed the fact that she really didn't have a handle on things. She was humiliated, and it ended a good business relationship between us. The other people in the company would never have asked the question like that. They would never have even called her into the meeting. I felt that my client pushed me into this situation, and it was hard to handle in a culturally appropriate way.

Jennifer Carey

Working across cultures can also give you a better understanding of how your own culture compares. Jim Nieters worked on a project that included an exchange of workshops between his company in California and another in Berlin. He ended up feeling that people in other countries were more receptive when people came to visit and more respectful of them as visitors. One example is that their notions of hospitality were different. When he arrived in Berlin, for example, someone met him and spent the evening with him. Then someone came to his hotel to walk him to the office and to dinners in the evening. But when it was his turn to host a workshop, he found it much harder to get his colleagues to participate. "What was interesting, when I was over there, I know everyone was busy, but even on a Friday afternoon there must have been 70 people there. When they came to our offices, it was difficult to get anyone to show up, and getting people to do anything outside of work was almost impossible. I spent some of my time with them, but no one else did. Even friends I would usually go out and have drinks with said 'No, I'm busy.' It's a curious thing."

Seeing Yourself Differently

In the end, experiencing new cultures helps you not only see them more clearly, but see yourself more clearly as well, broadening you as a person.

> The whole experience of living in Brussels for two years made me see how I had developed this particular filter, this way of seeing the world, through North American eyes. So often, I would interpret what I was seeing in terms of economics or efficiency. It really struck me how people from other cultures might have a very different way of interpreting the world. I met people who first and foremost thought in terms of its social relationships. I met someone who thought in terms of issues of art and culture. Many others had a strong sense of their place in history, and seemed to consider themselves actors in a story that stretched back hundreds of years. That was for me a pretty eye-opening experience—and the insight has stuck with me ever since.
>
> **Robert Barlow-Busch**

Being open to change in yourself is an important step for anyone in UX. It lets you be open to other people, and to allowing many experiences and cultures influence your design.

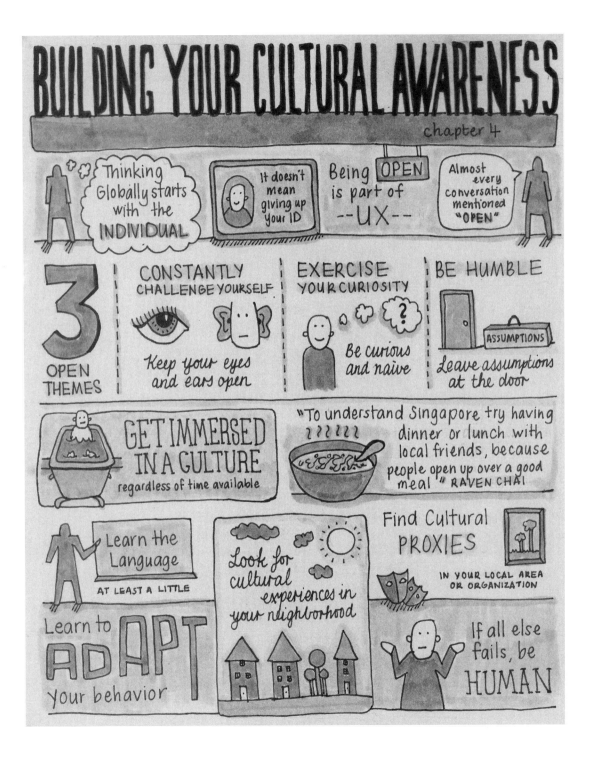

GLOBAL COMPANIES AND GLOBAL STRATEGY

IN THIS CHAPTER

In their weekly conference call Amit and Nils go over their plans to roll out new global web templates. Will they be able to do research and testing in enough markets? At least they have local offices around the world to work with. Kristin admires her new business cards. She loves that her company lets her choose a second language. Every time she sees the Arabic script, it reminds her that her company is global.

UX work is shaped by corporate structures and their strategy in an increasingly global world. It starts with defining different strategies for creating global products and then, how the different parts of the team work together. This includes specific product strategies, from a strong centrally managed brand to more regional variations and control.

As UX skills have evolved around the world, practitioners everywhere want more of a collaborative relationship and a stronger voice within the organization, in setting product direction. We hear this tension between central headquarters and the local regions as well as in tensions between UX teams at different levels of the company.

Not all companies want to be global. We will look at some companies that have chosen to be local and what that means for their perspectives.

- What kinds of global product strategies do companies pursue?
- What is the relationship between HQ and regional offices?

- What's the impact of offshoring, outsourcing, and local partnerships?
- How do I help my company think globally?
- Can a company choose to be local?

Organizations Have Cultures, Too

Just like any group of people, organizations have individual cultures that reflect their identity, goals, core values, and ways of working. An organization's culture both reflects and influences the policies, practices, and processes that are followed by individuals and work teams in an organization.

Companies may also bring their national culture to how they run their teams … and that affects how people work within that company, no matter where the office is located.

> My company is not your average local company. Even the Chinese on staff behave differently. The whole company culture is more western. Being a US company, we have a pretty open environment. We talk to our employees about decisions in an open way. But in local companies, often there is not this kind of discussion.
>
> **Dennis Kei Yip Poon**

Organizational Cultures Are All Different

Organizations develop their own practices and methods and processes but, as Kaleem Khan put it, culture is like the air you breathe, and can be difficult to identify from within. "The only time you realize how essential and omnipresent it is and how surrounding it is, is when you don't have it. Like air, people don't always consciously think about the impact of the organizational culture. It takes the ability to recognize that you are in an environment, that you're in an all-encompassing environment, to recognize the elements of what those things are, before you can even begin to attempt to make a change." This is as true within your own company as with markets and user groups.

Corporate culture brings assumptions. For example, a company can be focused on sales or research or technology. Working as a research scientist at Nokia, Rachel Hinman had to take the company culture into account as she planned her research, and address its underlying assumptions.

> An organization's culture deeply influences how people inside that organization see the world. It will inform their assumptions in ways they aren't even completely aware of. In a very technology-driven company, I had to start by understanding the context of

Connecting Cultures, Changing Organizations
Some conflict between the disciplines is a necessary part of the process. Another way to think of these conflicts is as checks and balances. They exist to help ensure that a product or service addresses customers' wants and needs, makes it to the marketplace on time, and has sufficient quality and robustness. Paul Sherman (2007)

the people in the organization. For example, Nokia is a very engineering-driven company. One of the activities I try to do at the beginning of any project is get the team to collectively identify our assumptions. I think it's important for everyone on the team to recognize the initial idea for a product or project has come to be and makes sense to us based on certain assumptions we have about the world. What are those assumptions? What is our level of confidence that those assumptions are right? How critical to the success of this project are we that our assumptions are correct?

Rachel Hinman

Even within a company, different disciplines from engineering to marketing to UX have their own cultural values. Their educational backgrounds and the demands of their work affect their approach to problem-solving and the value they place on specific activities. This can lead to miscommunication and conflict. Conflict is not always bad. The creative tension between perspectives can force a group into a more innovative strategy. It may be a necessary part of running any large company.

Four Global Product Strategies

The work of creating fully global products is a process that starts with the product concept. It starts with basic business questions like where you plan to sell the product and understanding the differences between that market and all the others.

Today's more connected world and the rise of the network makes companies that once might have been happily local to make decisions about how to respond to an international audience. This can be particularly difficult at both ends of the corporate spectrum:

- Large corporations may have grown into global companies without any overall strategy. For them, the challenge is to create a coherent user experience out of a confusing collection of local approaches.
- Small companies and start-ups have to make a conscious decision to build their products with internationalization and customization in mind.

Sometimes the market decides your strategy for you. Constant Contact was happy with its North American market, seeing itself as part of a single, large market. Then they noticed that they had a lot of customers accessing their services from Germany. Unfortunately, their software was not internationalized, so even creating a localized version in German was not going to be easy. Sarah Bloomer says the UX team worked "under the covers" to get the technical structures in place and be ready to meet their international audience. Kevin Cheng, working in California for companies such as Twitter and Yahoo, has noticed that more start-ups are taking a long view and considering an international audience from the beginning. Perhaps this is because so many start-ups are building purely digital products and services.

As we talked to people around the world, we heard a lot of different perspectives. It was hard to reconcile them until we thought about the different business relationships they represented. For example, we heard from people who were worried about losing their jobs to outsourcing, and also from people running thriving off-shore design and development companies.

We created a diagram showing the different relationships based on whether the UX team or the products were global.

	Where the products are used	
	One culture	Many cultures
Many locations	**Outsourcing: borrowed resources** Teams create products for other locations or cultures. Project is managed from a central points. Design are based on the culture of the target market.	**The flat world: multipoint collaboration** Teams may be located anywhere. Products are used in many places. Contributions to the design come from everywhere.
One location	**The local world: single point culture** Teams create products for their own cultures.	**Global reach: travel + local partners** A team from one place creates products used in many places. The design is controlled from a central location. Team members may travel for research insights or work with local partners.

(Vertical axis label: Where the UX team is located)

Figure 5.1 Global Corporate Relationships. The four quadrants of this diagram are a good starting point for talking about global companies and global products. Each quadrant represents a different relationship of the people who create a product and the people who use it. As companies become more global, they may follow any path through the different relationships.

- **The local world: A single point culture**
  Let's start with local products created by local teams. Of course, nothing really ever existed in this kind of pure isolation

(except in a diagram like this). Trade has always brought ideas from other cultures along with goods to sell. However, in this quadrant, the people who dream up and create the products are part of the culture in which they will be used. They can use their own cultural knowledge and their own patterns of behavior as models, learning about the user experience by using their own products in their own work or daily life. When the founder of Palm carried a block of wood in his pocket to test the size and weight, or when 37 Signals designs online tools that they use in their daily life, they are making use of their own experience to inform the design.

- **Outsourcing: Borrowed resources**
  Next is local products created by teams from many places. In the beginning, the UX work for products in this quadrant is no different from the local world. A local product and UX team manages the design and makes most of the decisions, or what Jhumkee Iyengar calls the "thinking work." The teams in other places may be "just hands" writing the code or doing the manufacturing, but more recently are designing product, too. They all have to adopt the cultural perspective of the target market for the many detailed decisions that affect user experience.

- **Global reach: Travel plus local partners**
  When a product is created in one culture, it can be pushed out to many different markets and cultures. Even if the manufacturing is outsourced, the concepts and user experience are designed in a single headquarters, such as the "multi-national" firms. These products have a wide range of globalization maturity. At one extreme, products designed for the local world are simply pushed out to other places. But more often, the company does at least some research on the culture of the places where they want to sell their products. For UX, this might mean a local team that travels to different places, or using local partners as informants to collect information about local culture and habits.

- **The flat world: Multipoint collaboration**
  Finally, we find teams around the world creating products for people in many different places. As the world gets more connected, mobile, and digital, it makes sense that companies want to sell more products in more places. Relationships that started out as off-shore development change when the outsourced resources become local informants and bring their own perspectives to the work. In UX, this multipoint collaboration is enabled by a maturing of skills around the world. The local partners who helped with international research for a global push become real partners, not just extensions of a central department.

The local world is the starting point for many companies. Outsourcing and global reach are two ways to extend past a single location or focus on a single country, but both are still rooted in a strong national orientation. The future looks more like the flat world, with collaboration and influence in all directions. This is not only Castells' networked world, but a connected age.

Another way to look at the relationships between companies or divisions within companies is how the collaborate for innovation.

Innovation Mall	Innovation Community	
A place where a company can post a problem, anyone can propose solutions, and they company chooses the solutions it likes best. *Example: InnoCentive.com website, where companies post scientific problems*	A network where anybody can propose problems, offer soutions, and decide which solutions to use. *Example: Linux open-source software community*	Open
Elite Circle	**Consortium**	
A select group of participants chosen by a company that also defines the problem and picks the solutions. *Example: Alessi's handpicked group of 200-plus design experts, who develop new concepts for home products*	A private group of participants that jointly select problems, decide how to conduct work, and choose solutions. *Example: IBM's partnerships with select companies to jointly develop semiconductor technologies*	Closed

GOVERNANCE

Hierarchical | Flat

Figure 5.2 Four ways to innovate and attract ideas from a wide variety of sources.
Pisano and Verganti (2008)

These ways of looking at corporate relationships and innovation collaborations both reflect degrees of openness and location of control:

- The Elite Circle and the Local World are both centralized views of the company.
- The Consortium and Global Reach rely on a closed set of partnerships.
- The Innovation Mall and Outsourcing reach out broadly, but with loose connections.
- The Innovation Community and the Flat World are both networks that allow contributions from any source.

Ready for Global Markets

The global market changes and shifts fast, so your software has to be planned with global markets in mind. If you don't build the flexibility into the architecture from the beginning, you can't be agile enough to move into markets when an opportunity arises. At Trend Micro, localization is a business strategy.

Hsin Eu's team is brought in early to assist with this process. Their work to adapt products for global markets is done on both a surface level and with deep customization.

The surface level of localization includes language and layout. This includes variations in the visual design, changes in layout, issues like designing for languages that read right-to-left, and language translations.

On a deeper level they also customize functionality and interaction. This can include deciding what functions will be included, as well as creating alternative versions of some functions. Their goal of maintaining a common code base takes a lot of planning.

These localization decisions are made before the design even starts. Typically, they customize only for their primary markets.

For other secondary markets they would only do the surface level localization, based on the global English version.

Making these decisions requires them to keep on top of their local markets. This knowledge is not isolated in one team, but is shared across departments. They start with internal expertise in the market, regularly summarizing local knowledge along with an analysis of the kinds of questions sales and support gets. They also do customer experience research to stay on top of trends and changes within each market. They catalog this information, so they can mine it for new projects easily and efficiently.

All of this allows them to get down to issues of different user or cultural expectations. For Hsin, this means understanding what users need in each country or environment. Finding that essence and translating into design is a key part of their work.

HQ and the Regions

In all the interviews, the relationship between headquarters and regional offices was fraught with the conflicts of perspectives of those in each part of the organization. This was especially true in companies that still maintain a strong control from a central office. Individual perspectives on this issue depended on where the person was located in the organization, and also on how well the company was doing in moving to the multipoint collaboration of the flat world. Even the short-hand terminology they use reflects this split.

- People who work outside of corporate headquarters feel a strong difference between themselves, and talk about *HQ, the central hub*, or *the mother ship*.
- People working from the center talk about *the regions* and *the markets*, as though they are abstract entities, instead of colleagues and equals.

The View Outside of Headquarters

Let's start with the people working outside of corporate headquarters. As local markets have grown, local teams move from simple outsourcing to being a regional office, and local UX skills matured, the frustration and strong desire for more influence and control is obvious. As several people put it, "The regions have no say," even though the reason there are teams focused on different geographical areas is to cater to local needs.

This is especially true for people who work in large companies. "Those companies tend to be very US-centric, especially in UX design. The web site is designed from the US and the UX personnel are always from the US HQ (or UK HQ)." Raven Chai sees a big split between them and the local staff who have no say in design. "That creates a lot of barriers for local staff. They are quite powerless to implement things they want to do because all the direction comes from HQ. There is no freedom to try new things out." Kevin Lee echoed this, saying that in his experience, "There's a tendency for nonheadquarters regions to be seen as second-level citizens. They don't get treated equally as how people treat each other in headquarters. They may accept that they will get rejected half the time, but will continue to try to bring attention to needs in their area."

Yu-Hsiu Li, the regional manager for a global computer manufacturer echoed that thought. "If you work for Ford, when we talk about the headquarters, everyone knows that's in the US. But if you are working in Asia, even when you try to do things the 'Asia way,' you also need to consider how the people in the HQ think about this region." The real problems, however, come when decisions have to be made. One way to do this is for headquarters to just make all the decisions. But they cannot fully understand what is going on in this region, so they need their local offices to report back the reality in each area. Ideally, they will incorporate everyone's opinion, building a global consensus. Unfortunately, the reality is not always so progressive. "Since we both work for the same company, normally we would be equal. But in the globalization, who's opinion is more important. So are decisions made just based on who has the authority? We all know that is very risky."

Mark Webster also saw this from his positions as running offices in Hong Kong, Vietnam, Thailand, Philippines, and Japan for an international brand and marketing agency. From his perspective in an advertising agency, he sees a difference between luxury brands that tend to have a single brand image around the world, and household products that have more local variation.

> People understand that they work with a global company, but they are working with a local client, selling products in a local market, so they sort of resent anything coming from the center. When you talk about cross-cultural communication … it's just human nature to dislike things that are being forced on you or sent from somewhere else. Part of my challenge was to get that healthy balance. 'Don't look at head office as the bad guys,' I'd say. 'They are doing it that way for a reason, and we need to do it this way locally for another reason,' and then we'd find the right balance for a satisfactory solution.
>
> **Mark Webster**

Of course, any individual's degree of influence and access is partly based on their position in the company. A design manager in Beijing will be able to contribute on a more strategic level than a team member; their managers, one level up, will have even more exposure and influence.

When Michael De Regt moved from the Philips head office in the Netherlands to China, he found that "even communicating with Eindhoven is different because I am 7 hours ahead. It's different for me to be so far from the place where many decisions are being made, especially decisions that can have an influence on our work. When you are in the head office, you don't notice anything special about being there, but as soon as you go to Hong Kong, you can feel the resentment and the trouble people have with being managed from a distance."

It's easy to talk about companies as though all headquarters are in North America or Europe, but there are Indian and Asian multinational companies, too. Think about Infosy, Wipro,

Samsung, Huawei, LG, Haier, or Lenovo to name just a few. The challenge of managing the relationships between regional offices and headquarters applies to any global company.

Maintaining a Global Brand

Another perspective comes from people responsible for managing a consistent brand for a global product, even with local variations. This raises questions about corporate structure and organization, as well as design strategy: do you have a single template? How much variation is too much? What kind of differences are appropriate?

At HSBC, web sites have grown up in 86 countries with no consistency in design or functionality. "Our challenge," Kimberly Wiessner told us, "is to provide a vision for products that takes in considerations from all over the globe. Our challenge is to find the areas where we can align things, and start to set some internal best practice for how we design things around customer needs."

Managing global UX from a central HQ takes a lot of work and strong control. Like several people we talked to, Chris Rourke has often worked with this type of organization. "They have to be aware of the issues internationally, and see if differences are causing variances in use or sales, and why. They are having to rely on their local office to be their eyes and ears in that country and give them evidence of where the problems are, and how to fix them. One of our roles has been to help the central hub understand local, and bring back good qualitative information that they might not be aware of."

This is partly because "UX is no longer tucked away in an e-commerce team, but is becoming almost as important as brand. As UX gets higher on the radar, it's more important to control it, but you still have to make sure that everything is fit for purpose in the local markets."

Getting teams in different regions to work together toward a shared vision is not easy, especially when the teams and expertise are spread out. It takes a lot of communication and time to work through the cultural and historical *baggage* that each country brings. Itamar Medeiros, a Brazilian working in China, also says that "Westerners don't always realize how different Asian cultures are, because western culture is very homogeneous in terms of shared references, no matter how many different countries there are."

One thing that seems to help is cross-functional teams, with people from the technology, business, and design sides all working closely together. Often, these teams are also cross-cultural, bringing together people from different locations to work on a product. Despite the challenge of managing a global team, the added diversity in both the culture and skills disciplines is an advantage. Working in a company that instituted cross-functional teams, Dennis Kei Yip Poon felt that everyone was able to contribute at a more strategic level because there is a very flat communication structure within the teams.

Global Partnerships

Another aspect of global products that raised a lot of emotions in the interviews is the question of outsourcing and off-shoring. Concerns about "shipping jobs overseas" usually meaning "to emerging markets" have been widely discussed in the general media and business press in the West.

The economic and social implications of the globalization of work is a bigger question than we can tackle in this book. It's easy to see it as simply competition for jobs. But for UX, it's also an expansion of the number of practitioners around the world and an opportunity for all of them to work on the same range of projects. One person we talked to wondered whether someone from China is really the best UX designer for a US market. "I've worked around Chinese people in the US my whole adult life, but I still don't think I know enough to design for that culture." Turn their statement around, and it's obvious that someone from the United States might not be the best designer for China, either.

> **Globalization: Curse or Blessing?**
>
> It is possible that globalisation could promote labour market flexibility to such an extent that employment rises in the long run. If so, globalisation will not be a curse for employment in Western Europe; it could instead turn out to be a blessing. (CESifo 2008)

Two Sides to Outsourcing

UX designers like to think that their work can't be sent outside their own company, let alone off-shore. A panel on outsourcing and off-shoring at the CHI 2005 conference took a fairly predictable view that you can't outsource UX because "HCI work is best done by individuals within close geographical proximity to the key individuals who provide input into the product design: senior managers, marketing, sales, and of course the end user."

In a 2004 article reflecting on the impact of outsourcing on UX, Aaron Marcus reflected on the impact of outsourcing on UX and summed it up this way:

> Discussions about the effects of outsourcing on the future of our professional lives seem to be binary. Some dismiss the likelihood that off-shore design and usability professionals will loosen North American and European professionals' hold on product and service development. Others seem anxious and pessimistic about the impending collapse of jobs and markets for their services. Both speak of "core competencies" in Western businesses. But what are

these exactly? Of the basic user-interface development tasks, which ones are impervious to cheaper overseas labor: planning, research, analysis, design, implementation, evaluation, documentation, training, or maintenance?

Aaron Marcus

Just a few years later, he noticed that some of the designers he met at conferences in India and Asia had projects in their portfolio that his own firm had bid on.

But look from the other side, and we heard about the frustration of being a "back office" instead of an equal part of the team. Samir Chabukswar recalled being told, "We'll do the thinking, and you do the work." This was partly being viewed primarily as cheap labor, but also "because there was not great user experience design talent in India at that time" (around 2002–2004).

> I worked with an off-shoring company for four years. Projects came through a pipeline somewhere and landed on your desk. You can't connect to the user. You can't connect to the client. You can't talk to anyone. Just create the design and send it. The big decisions are going to be made wherever the project came from.

> I would call it ridiculous because we are working in the field of user experience. Maybe in some other field, this would make sense, but in user experience, it's almost silly. But I am a real pragmatic, and I understand how business functions, and at the end of the day a product has to go out the door. So, I rose to the occasion and at the end of the two weeks, I made something. I made assumptions, and I used equivalent users in India to do some testing. At the end of the day, you try to do justice to the work. But being a back office sets the direction for a lot of the work in this environment.

> **Jhumkee Iyengar**

> **The Moment of Truth**
> You may try to stop UX design from off-shoring. You may also help nurture UX expertise abroad, to bring it up to the standards we thrive to maintain at home. Collaboration and partnership on equal grounds is the only effective way to move forward in the truly global economy. Lada Gorlenko (2006)

Adapting UX Practices for Off-Shore Work

Work on off-shore projects might have been some of the first internationally distributed UX projects. Like any global team, off-shore teams have to coordinate staff in several locations.

One solution is some travel. Eric Shaffer, head of Human Factors International, with offices around the world including Asia, Europe, and the United States, wrote in a 2006 article that "We have found that the best practice requires travel and blending of staff. Over 80 percent of our projects blend local staff with global resources. The local staff understand the nuances of culture and language. They are also easily present for design meetings. Generally we figure one-third of the hours worked on a project will be done by local staff."

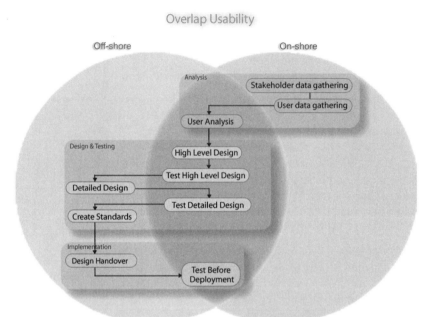

Figure 5.3 Overlap Usability. Facing the challenges of conceptual, geographical and methodological, culture and time zone separations between the end user and their development environment, Overlap Usability adapted a user-centered design methodology to work in the off-shoring environment, placing critical tasks on-shore, off-shore, or in a blended environment Samir Chabuskwar (2007) mapped different arrangements for companies at different stages of maturity in a poster "Practical Approach to Usability Practice in the Off-shore Development Space." A presentation with Jhumkee Iyengar (2008) "Moving from Usability Oblivion to a Thriving Off-shore Usability Practice" explored the issues in managing projects in more detail.

Changing Attitudes

UX leaders in India and other Asian countries have sometimes had to fight for respect, but the experience of working with global products and growing opportunities for UX education locally is increasing interest in UX, and producing a growing number of professionals with good training.

> Indian designers thought that they were just supposed to listen and do what they are told. They often did things without thinking. "Hey, the CEO wants pink color because his wife likes pink—give it to him." That same kind of design culture showed up in software design, too. But as an awareness that design is not just something based on the whims and fancies of the decision makers grew, we began to push back. Now Indian designers are finding the balance between the scientific and the creative, performing to expectations of customers, and also trying to push the boundaries of good design.
>
> **Samir Chabukswar**

As a result, people in Asian countries are starting to recognize local talent. "Not so long ago (in the early 2000s) Westerners in Asia seemed to get an extra measure of respect simply because they were Western. But that is changing." Raven Chai believes that in Singapore (if not more widely), people are starting to judge expertise on its own merits rather than by its source. He sees two reasons for this shift:

- In the macro view, there is progress made by Singapore as a whole, and that provides a measure of general confidence. Singapore has made some landmarks in the international scene.
- In the micro view, there are more and more global companies and business leaders coming from Singapore. This gives us confidence that we have been taking the right things from the United States and the right values from the Chinese.

They are also finding a way to blend both Chinese and Western approaches to business. He says, "We have adopted the American way of running a business based on merit, but our relationships are very much in an Asian style. We like to build long-term relationships to understand each other. We start by asking if we think alike. Then, we can invest time to become better friends and better business partners. Only when we have gotten to know a person's thoughts do we trust them."

OUTSOURCING CAN BRING CREATIVE IDEAS TO A CORPORATE CULTURE

The furniture company Herman Miller partners a furniture company with external designers for all new product development, and has for over 70 years. It takes work to create the conditions for success, but they have worked to create a corporate culture that "actively engages with and, in fact, welcomes the participation of an external designer."

The benefits:

- Outside designers bring a diversity of ideas.
- Designers might be located anywhere, bringing different world views.
- The company has the flexibility to select a designer with the right expertise and passion for each project.
- As outsiders, the designers are more likely to think outside of the corporate envelope for new ideas.
- The designers are less likely to compromise too early to maintain internal corporate good will.

(Kenneth Munch's 2004 article Outsourcing design and innovation, is a case study of design management.)

Off-Shore Work, Cross-Cultural Team, International Users

Sometimes a project is global in many different ways. One off-shore (India and US) project that Samir Chabukswar worked on crossed both national and work cultures, with an audience of international users.

The product was a life-sciences medical research application with end users in labs across the United States, Europe, Australia, China, and Singapore. "Initially neither I nor my fellow designers could really understand what this was supposed to be about because none of us are like doctors in a medical field. Everybody came from a design background or engineering, so the tricky part was to understand the domain."

At the beginning of the project, the design team spent about three months in the United States acquiring enough domain knowledge to understand the product. "As we talked to these MD/PhD doctors, we realized that no way do we have enough domain knowledge to conduct the initial user interviews. So, we trained the customer to work with us to elicit user requirements and user needs, in medical language. We created the interview plan, but the customer was the one to ask the questions, because he could speak the language of genetics research."

They had a creative process that mixed on-shore and off-shore staff. In this situation, having a designer near the users was really important. "By being able to visit the labs, we learned about their entire work day, not just how they would interact with the software we were designing. I wouldn't have got that if I was only working from India."

The most important part of the job for people with the client in the United States is to keep in touch with the designers in India with daily briefings. These covered more than just answers to the questions, but everything that they observed. The success of this approach really depends on the researcher's sensitivity in capturing contextual details from the users and then the communication skills to feed this information back into the project.

Ultimately, the goal is to merge everyone into a single team. As Samir put it, "The point is that you are team-mates, no matter where you sit. The communication process has to be built in at every stage."

UX in the Organization

There is still a large gap between the companies where UX is still unknown and those where it has become part of daily life. At one extreme are the companies who still don't do any UX. There's not much about them in this book, simply because there are no UX people there to talk to.

At the other extreme are companies, often design agencies, that have completely adopted UX. As one designer put it, "doing research is part of the core DNA of our company." In between are companies who do a little UX—perhaps a single quick user research project, or where some departments are more engaged than others.

The reality is that the adoption of UX is uneven, but many people talked about a transition as businesses became more interested in finding ways to understand their customers better, and to provide a better experience. This trend may be partly because these projects are run by marketing and e-commerce groups rather than IT departments. As they enter new markets, or introduce new products, they want a high level of confidence in their research and design decisions.

Managing Global UX Teams

Even in organizations with established UX teams, there are continued challenges, both within the UX teams and in working with the larger company. Some of these issues are the same as managing the user experience within any company: finding a voice within the company, coordinating work between teams, and keeping up with the rapid pace of digital markets. But UX leaders in global companies face an additional layer of challenges. They may not have strong connections between multiple UX teams, or may even have outright conflict between them.

A challenge for creating a coherent view of the global UX in a large company is the way so many companies are organized in silos. Working from a consultancy in Asia, Maria Sit sees the impact of these silos.

> The current organizational structure of many global firms is arranged around product lines, segments, and specific channels. The resulting silos make it very difficult to align and coordinate UX effort across the organization for creating a coherent multichannel customer experience. This also has direct impact on staff (customer facing and back office) whose experience as users of

various internal systems is sometimes shocking. Their ability to deliver an optimized experience for their customers is severely hampered. Siloed organizations breed siloed experiences. Thankfully, some organizations are tackling this head-on by integrating UX techniques as part of their effort to overhaul some of their systems that support both their staff and customers' interactions.

Maria Sit

UX as a Change Agent

UX often serves as a *natural liaison*, what Adam Polansky (2006) calls people who bridge gaps between functional areas, enabling communication between groups, and mitigating conflict and its consequences. Many of the people interviewed for this book have crossed boundaries, for example, in bringing strong technical knowledge and language skills to internationalization or simply bringing their own experience of several cultures to a project. In doing so, they span both organizational and social cultural divides and help move organizations from the status quo to a better, more communicative and collaborative state.

Sometimes UX has an explicit role in changing the culture of an organization. Peter Grierson's work was typical of the UX team-of-one, taking on a 10-year developer legacy of an engineering-centric process as he introduces UCD to the company. "My goal is to adjust the culture, not to come in and take over. I'm starting with individuals, keeping everyone involved in the process." In other companies, UX can help drive change. Jeff Eddings saw the power of having an explicit role for UX in defining products when he worked as a product manager at Google.

> There's a lot of talk about culture within companies, and there's a couple of factors that can affect UX and how it's received within the organization. It's not just a matter of writing down a cultural statement. It comes down to leaders setting the tone from the top of the company. It's also "put your money where your mouth is." At Google, there was a very specific group of people structured around UX. It was a team hired and created to do just that. And they weren't tucked away in some corner doing UX work that no one ever saw, but were integrated into the engineering team … Where the team was located said a lot about what kind of products they were trying to create, and the role of UX in doing that.

Jeff Eddings

UX managers also have an opportunity to ensure that UX includes strong global perspectives. Support for design research can still be hard, and making the case for international travel even harder. One approach is to build on any opening, such as a request for help from one region. Tomer Sharon says that this sometimes starts as a local issue that he can use as the basis for a global project. "It doesn't start as global—it becomes global when I do the planning." Others talked about having a strong enough portfolio that they start a project from a position of trust and don't have to spend too much time convincing people.

Invest in People

I joined Citix to bring user experience to a company that had not invested in this process. This was brand new for the majority of the product organization. As a result there was a lot of simultaneous education and doing. One of the things that drew me to this new opportunity was the fact that I would be collaborating with a global organization. As a company that's mission is to enable people to "work or play from anywhere," I though that was an exciting element of the position.

In my first 90-days on the job, I invest heavily in reaching out to people throughout the organization. I knew I could not expect people to find me, so I spent as much time as I could meeting people throughout the company. I met with leaders of product management, but found that it was also important to meet executives from other divisions. I wanted all parts of the organization to be aware of why the company was investing in this new user experience effort.

Citrix has numerous products to enable affective remote collaboration. Now, I use them daily to work with team. But in my first few months, I took the extra time to meet everyone in person. I felt it was important to demonstrate the importance of these meetings by taking the time to travel. I was certain it would make for a much better and more memorable discussion if done in person.

By visiting offices in other locations I was also able to get a better sense of the culture and how it varies from location to location around the globe. This was a surprise to me and an important insight I would not have gained if I only met people over the phone. Now I try and maintain a personal relationship by connecting "face-to-face" using our HD Faces collaboration technology.

I believe that making the early investment face-to-face has made for much better long-term remote working relationships.

Catherine Courage

Managing Corporate Politics

Outside the UX teams, it's important to find ways to be part of the conversation at a more strategic level. Some companies are (finally) starting to introduce customers much earlier in their process. In a large company or financial institutions, this can be a big change. For business partners, customer input can now be part of the rationale for change. No matter how mature the company is, integrate yourself into the larger product and business teams, instead of focusing entirely on UX work. One advantage is that you hear about opportunities earlier.

> I try to attend as many meetings outside of the UX world as possible, so I can listen for things that are being said by different people, or by similar people in different contexts. And then, there is a lightbulb flashing and saying here's an opportunity for a research project, or a knowledge gap that I can fill in. Being in the meetings means that I can plant seeds that may lead to a research project later.
>
> **Tomer Sharon**

Another advantage is that you learn more about the perspectives of other stakeholders, and may even find yourself moving into a more strategic role in the company.

The bottom line for consultancies is that starting a new research program requires that the client trust you. Global research may be more expensive or take more time than they are used to. Or, they may be just starting to think about getting more depth in their research. Bill DeRouchey suggests a process that builds on success, staring with a small project. "They saw the value at a smaller level, which opened up their eyes to tackling it at a bigger level. It would be far more challenging, I think, for any company with any client to do this on the first shot."

UX Can Make a Difference

When introducing UX or making UX more global requires a company to change, it can be hard. According to Kaleem Khan the best way to motivate people to undertake a change, whether it's a cultural change or a change in practice or process, is to make it part of the goals against which they are evaluated. The real payoff is not in a single project, but in long-term change. "It's a new way of working and a new way of thinking," Janna DeVylder, from Meld Consulting, told us. "It's about how what you are doing is influencing the internal workings of the company. In the absence of that, it's not sincere and it will fail."

Choosing to Be Local

Two people we talked to are from companies aiming to be local. Both see their role as being leaders to help develop UX in their own country to word-class status.

Trent Mankelow is a founder of Optimal Usability, based in New Zealand. In his view, to be able to do the best work in their own country, they have to have a good understanding of work around the world. They make a point of going to overseas conferences and staying in touch with their largely international customers for the Optimal Workshop tools for user research (http://www.optimalworkshop.com).

One problem he sees is that designers can be insecure about New Zealand's place in the world, despite the innovative work being done there. Some of that work builds on their deep local knowledge; he was impressed that the CEO's vision for KiwiBank was to win the race for the best financial management tools by using their deep knowledge of their customers.

Even with a focus on a small country like New Zealand, they can see differences. For example, on a project for the University of Canterbury web site, they saw that people in Christchurch, where the university is located, used the site differently than people in Auckland. Features like photos of the campus were more valuable to people from other cities. It can be difficult to be so close to the products and audience, "because it's like describing water you are swimming in."

Raven Chai is another UX consultant who has made a deliberate choice to be local. After working for a global consultancy, he decided to focus on his home in Singapore. Working with local clients had many advantages for him. Being local is a differentiator when he competes for work. He can win projects, even against global "names," because he can speak to the local situation. The clients trust a local consultant and have let him try new ideas because it is easy for them to communicate and keep the decision-making process collaborative. Best of all, it gives him more freedom to work, without taking direction from a global HQ.

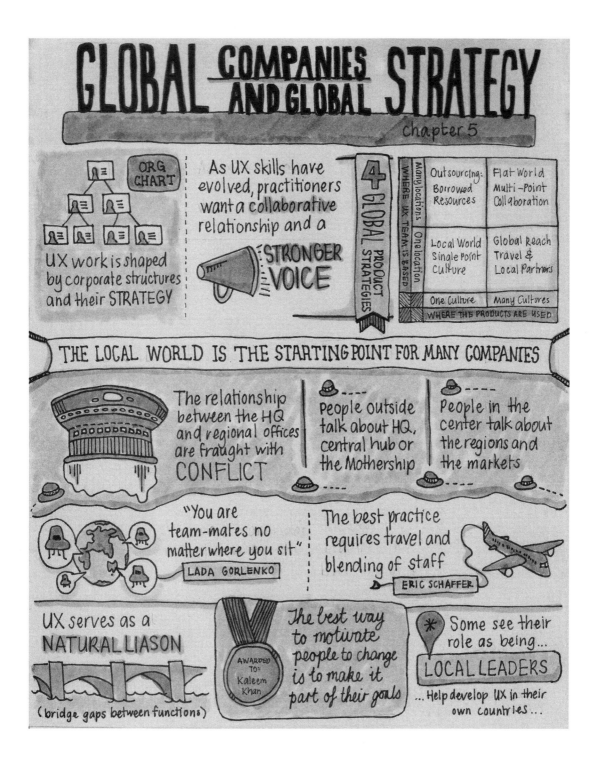

GLOBAL COMPANIES AND GLOBAL STRATEGY

chapter 5

ORG CHART

UX work is shaped by corporate structures and their STRATEGY

As UX skills have evolved, practitioners want a collaborative relationship and a STRONGER VOICE

4 GLOBAL PRODUCT STRATEGIES

WHERE UX TEAM IS BASED			
	Many locations	Outsourcing: Borrowed Resources	Flat World Multi-Point Collaboration
	One location	Local World Single Point Culture	Global Reach Travel & Local Partners
		One Culture	Many Cultures
		WHERE THE PRODUCTS ARE USED	

THE LOCAL WORLD IS THE STARTING POINT FOR MANY COMPANIES

The relationship between the HQ and regional offices are fraught with CONFLICT

People outside talk about HQ, central hub or the Mothership

People in the center talk about the regions and the markets

"You are team-mates no matter where you sit"
LADA GORLENKO

The best practice requires travel and blending of staff
ERIC SCHAFFER

UX serves as a NATURAL LIASON

(bridge gaps between functions)

AWARDED TO: Kaleem Khan

The best way to motivate people to change is to make it part of their goals

Some see their role as being...
LOCAL LEADERS
...Help develop UX in their own countries...

6

EFFECTIVE GLOBAL TEAMS

Arriving at work, Katrin checks her e-mail and finds a set of wireframes for a series of pages she's been working on with Malik. She has several hours before he's up, so she sketches a few notes in the margin and posts them for comments by other people on the team. By the time he pings her for a call, she's also checked in with another researcher working on a similar problem.

Global companies and global products mean global teams. And global teams bring new challenges for both leading the team and supporting collaboration among team members. We've reached the point in our journey when it's time to look inside global UX projects and see what makes them tick along so well.

If there is one message we heard loud and clear, it is, "Communicate, communicate, communicate." Bridging time and distance, different working practices, and communication styles is an ongoing task. "There are more moving parts, and plenty to go wrong," Tim Loo, Director of Consulting at Foolproof, says.

We'll hear how people running global UX teams organize their group, support and nurture their team members, and structure their work.

We'll look at the many different ways practitioners have adapted to life as part of a global team and the techniques and tools they use to manage working at a distance. Some of the challenges are practical, some address issues of cross-cultural collaboration, some speak to the nature of UX work itself.

- How are successful global UX teams organized?
- How do global teams manage time zones and physical distance?
- How do teams communicate across language and cultural differences?
- How do teams add to—and take advantage of—their UX and cross-cultural knowledge?

Organizing a Global UX Team

There are many patterns for setting up global teams. The list of arrangements we heard about was almost as varied as the number of people we spoke to. In many cases the configuration of the team was carefully thought out; in others it was based on a combination of convenience and happenstance.

All the teams in this book are, to some extent, global teams. But, the degree to which the team *felt* global was based partly on the individual's role. As the only usability person from his company in Taiwan, Yu-Hsiu Li is the representative of a whole region and feels the global nature of the work strongly. "Every project I work on is global—all my colleagues are all over the world. Especially because our headquarters is in the US, and my manager is based in Austin."

We talked to teams for products sold around the world, but because corporate culture was so strongly local, it was hard to keep the global audience in mind. Other teams were melting pots, with people from many different cultures working together, sometimes on local products.

But not every project is global. We also heard from people who worked in companies based in one country who did not face issues of "being global" in their day-to-day work.

Central UX Groups

For many companies, the work of global research and setting UX standards falls to a central team. Typically, their role is to work at a strategic level on new UX challenges, or creating templates that are lightly adapted for regional sites.

A few have one team, located at the company headquarters or largest market. They work with regional partners and outside companies for research and design. In some cases much of their own travel is virtual; in others, research managers travel to check in with or be part of their projects. Even centralized teams usually include at least a few people from different parts of the world. They are often assembled organically, with people added to a central team from wherever they are located.

The future looks both global and interdisciplinary, bringing divergent viewpoints into a single team. Kevin Lee runs a virtual global team of designers, content designers, and people from marketing who define the user experience, features, and solutions for eBay sites around the world including the United States, United Kingdom, Europe, and Asia. "This is an interdisciplinary team of people who believe in driving a global level effort on user experience." One of their goals is to create a shared understanding of cultural differences around the world, and then look for a way to converge on solutions that are not so different, allowing room for the regional teams to take some ownership, too.

Global Offices for Functional Groups

One of the most common patterns we heard about is having teams organized into offices by function. These companies might have their corporate headquarters in the United States; development groups in China, India, and Germany; and UX groups in the United States, Asia, and Europe. These offices are placed strategically, in key markets, or to take advantage of talent in a particular area.

We talked to the head of a design group in Shanghai that handles a portfolio of 150 software products for both the international and local China markets. His company wanted teams located in key markets, but also wanted the team for a set of products to be colocated. When Doug Wang started the office, his mission was to establish a team that could integrate into a global operation in Singapore, San Francisco, and Switzerland. As he built his team, he started hiring locally in Shanghai, where he found both Chinese and expatriate designers. Then he moved some people from India and Singapore to join the team. Each project has a different balance of global and local requirements, so his resource pool has to be flexible enough to assemble the right team for each project. He says, "This mix of people can deliver high quality products because we can sync internationally and come from many cultural backgrounds. We have to understand what people want around the planet, as well as understanding the specific business and engineering disciplines the products are for."

The desire to have a team largely based in one place can be driven by the wish for easy collaboration within the UX group, to enable cross-functional collaboration, or to be near the company decision-makers. The Customer Experience Technology Team for HSBC, a bank with locations in 86 countries, has team members located with their primary business stakeholders at the biggest offices (in this case, Chicago, Vancouver, London, and Hong Kong).

Consultancies also create offices to be near their clients or markets. Mark Webster, for example, managed country offices of a global brand consultancy, each focused on serving their local market. When Adaptive Path, a UX design company based in San Francisco, opened their second office in Amsterdam, they made a deliberate decision to hire people with a lot of experience working and living in different countries. Their first five people all lived in Amsterdam, but they included people from the United States, Sweden, and Netherlands.

> I worked with a client a few years ago who had a very international design team. They were represented from all corners of the earth. I thought, if I'm going to do this international thing, that's what I want it to look like. It just felt right. And so, as we've been building out, I am looking for folks from all over. First and foremost, they have to be really good designers. Folks who have gone out of their natural habitat tend to be the good ones.
>
> **Henning Fischer**

Face Time for Virtual Teams

Being based in many locations doesn't mean that a team never gets to work together. It's easier to generate ideas and make decisions when a team is in one place. Some companies have built this into the structure of their work. Many consultancies we talked to have their main design group in a single location, but have researchers are all over, selected based on the location of the client or countries they are interested in for any project. Some bring the researchers back to their office to work with the design group for critical times in their process, but others manage these relationships remotely.

On a project for a global manufacturer with offices in New York and Hong Kong, Josh Seiden worked both remotely and in person with team members in each location. The time spent together made the remote collaboration easier

> One thing that worked well was that they built a project team that was really representative of all of the different offices and that it

was pretty successfully cross functional. We had people on the project team from both offices. We have business analysts, developers, and designers on the team. We all spent a lot of time traveling. There was rarely a moment on the project when someone from one office was not working in the other office. The New York team was often sending people to go to Hong Kong for two weeks. And the Hong Kong offices were often sending people to New York for two week stretches. That built a level of relationship on the project that made it very easy when you weren't there, to pick up the phone and call and say what's going on.

Josh Seiden

Teams can also grow into multidisciplinary groups. Bas Raijmakers and Geke van Dijk ran a company focused on design research until they wanted to be able to work in a more integrated way. "We decided to team up with designer companies and technology-focused companies, programmers, to really become part of multidisciplinary teams. We had already been working with other companies with these skills and projects, but it's never as close as we wanted because you have to send invoices all the time, so we were really happy to be able to join forces with several of these companies and actually turned into a large company that would take all kinds of interactive projects—kind of full service."

Working Globally

Finally, some teams are fully global, with people around the world functioning as a single group. Tomer Sharon's team at Google is a good example. The UX team for his product has people in the US west coast, US east coast, United Kingdom, Shanghai, and Tokyo. The engineering and product management team adds even more countries. As he put it, "I've internalized this so much that I'm not even thinking about it. The team is global. There is no Shanghai team or London team. The team is for the product, and you work together. The only thing that bothers us as I'm sure many others is time zones, but we're flexible, so we try to overcome that. It's so natural to me that I'm not sure what to say."

Dealing with Distance

The economic world may be getting flatter, but the earth is still round, so long-distance relationships and time zones are a fact of life for global work. Everyone still struggles with creating and maintaining good, easy, working relationships over distance. Even when the internal UX group is located in a single place, they usually need to work with people around the world including colleagues in regional offices and local research or design partners.

No one had a perfect answer to this challenge. Instead, every group has put together a set of tools and habits they use to make it work. For many, there is a constant struggle to find ways for our teams to communicate well, relying on a variety of tools from simple phone calls to shared workspaces. One factor in the choice of how to communicate is creating the best connection between the people involved.

> When you are talking about design in particular, there is nothing that matches being *with* someone. So, if you can't be there, then we always encourage people to pick up the phone and talk to people rather than sending an e-mail. And video conference rather than telephone. You learn more on a telephone call than you do on a sequence of e-mails. When we think about what gives us the best connection, it's video call vs telephone call vs e-mail vs message board.
>
> **Giles Colborne**

Of course, some of these issues are true for any distributed team. Consultants and agencies are almost always working on distributed teams with their clients. "We are never involved in something that is all created in one place. We are grappling with the same problems, whether there is an overseas element or not," Giles Colborne told us.

Christine Petersen, who coaches teams on communication skills, reminds us that "Teamwork is about good communication, motivation, and engagement—not many people are motivated or engaged by an e-mail especially when it arrives with another 120 e-mails." One problem she sees is that with all the collaboration tools available today, there is very little agreed best practice and process on how we work together as teams.

Collaboration across Distance

Working at a distance means you have to be more aware of including everyone. When UX is separate from the main product team it can be especially difficult, because not being colocated can mean getting left out of conversations.

Communication can also be a challenge. At one company where Hsin Eu worked, the US R&D center in the United States included people from six different countries (Ukraine, India, US,

China, Taiwan, and Greece). They collaborated with a second center in India. "The remote collaboration was hard, partly because of the accents. We didn't have great collaboration technology and sometimes the phone lines weren't very good. It was hard to understand their points sometimes, and hard to know whether they got our points. It was hard for everyone."

This happens at the organizational or team level, especially when UX is structured as a service organization, and not part of the core product team. At one company, Jhilmil Jain found that "Because we are not all in one location, a number of critical meetings happen that we are not part of. For example, if you are talking about brand perception, UX people need to be in the conversation, but when we are not right there, they don't think to include us."

Some approaches to design and development practically demand that the team be in the same place. If your work relies on large quantities of sticky notes and big wall surfaces, everyone needs to be able to see that wall. A manager from a development company in India put it simply, "Distance work is challenging for Agile." Darci Dutcher, a UX designer who works with Agile teams, tried using an electronic substitute for the card wall, but found that "it's not as satisfying as moving real cards around. On one project where I was not physically with the team, I created my own card wall and I would physically update it to match."

Even with good intentions, it's hard to include people who aren't *right there* in the impromptu hallway conversations that are part of any collaborative work. Distance can be relative, however. For some, being on different floors of a building can seem just as far away as being across the world. Some of the stories we heard about teams having difficulty collaborating over distance included people as close as down the hall, or a seemingly short drive away. Any successful virtual collaboration has to find a way to bridge that distance.

Sharing the Time-Zone Pain

The other challenge of global distances is that someone is always getting up very early or staying up late to join a meeting. Even people who were working in fully global teams mentioned this, often as the most difficult practical problem. If you have people in Asia, Australia, Europe, and both sides of the United States, you can't have a meeting with everyone at the same time.

They also pointed out that companies don't always prioritize who is doing the time shifting well. Some work this out collaboratively, with each side shifting slightly to create more overlap without penalizing anyone too much; others are not as thoughtful about it.

If you are managing research or design vendors around the world, it can fall to you to adjust to time zones. None of the research managers we talked to kept to a 9-to-5 schedule. It was just too hard to keep up with projects without being flexible. For example, as one of a pair of global research managers, based in California, Jim Hudson and his colleague built a consideration of time zones into how they structured their work. They divide up the world, with one managing work in Europe and the other handling Asia-Pacific, to reduce the number of time zones they each have to cross in their daily work.

> We've got a system that works pretty well, at least for me. I get up early every morning and deal with phone calls from home because that's the end of the day in Europe or the middle of the day in Latin America. It works pretty well because I'm at home making calls until mid-morning, so when I drive into the office, it's after rush hour—that's a plus. I really do try to leave the office by 4 PM. I may do some work from home.
>
> It was more of a struggle for my colleague who manages our research in A-PAC since we frequently contract with a large research vendor headquartered in Europe. With this arrangement, she found her self on both early morning and late night calls. I know that it was a struggle for her to fit this into her family's schedule. Fortunately, a little flexibility from everyone involved has allowed her to settle into a rhythm that works for her.
>
> **Jim Hudson**

When the internal team is spread around the world, this means negotiating habits that make it possible to work together. In many cases, the headquarters office, often in the United States or Europe, would schedule meetings during their work day. This meant that people in Asia or India were staying up to make calls at 1:30 in the morning. But in more recent years, attitudes are shifting to sharing the pain. Jim Nieters described how this shift took place at his company.

> Our meetings with our team in India used to all be scheduled in the US morning. With Bangalore 12 or 13 and a half hours ahead, no matter what time I meet with them, if it's daylight here, it's the middle of the night for them. So it's much better to meet with them in my evening, so it's mid-morning for them. Three years ago, we really didn't care that we were asking colleagues to meet with us in the middle of the night.

Now, we are more likely to respect their time concerns more. No one told us to, but as we recognize that they are a partner and collaborator, we see them more as part of our team. When that happens, we naturally think more about their lives and are more flexible to make sure the meeting times work for them as well as for us. That's a shift away from that old arrogance that 'You have to meet on our time.' It is still there: they would never ask us to meet at 1:30 in the morning, and we do still ask them to do this sometimes. But it's shifting.

Jim Nieters

This move to make everyone more equal pays off in better working relationships. When people are separated by more than 8 hours, someone has to give up some time outside of 9-to-5 business hours, either early in the morning or late in the evening. Being willing to accept some of that pain is one way to set up a good relationship. Kevin Lee finds that when he is the one setting up a meeting, he gets a better response when he is willing to accommodate their schedule. "It's more of a service model when you try to serve them versus having them serve you."

In the Same Place … for Key Moments

Establishing trust and a smooth working relationship can be difficult at a distance. As part of this process, there's nothing like being in the same place for key moments. A common team pattern is to get together either on a regular schedule or at critical moments during a project, such as the kickoff, the transition from research to design, and at important design milestones. Being able to meet the people you are working with just changes the tone of the whole relationship because you understand who you are working with. This travel can pay off in future working relationships.

I've been investing a lot this year in spending that time with vendors face to face. There is a period of time in which you get to know people. Then, when we do have conversations over the phone or over Skype, or even through (text) chat, you've got a really good sense of who that person is. You understand their humor. You've spent a good deal of time with that person. At the end of the day, we're all people so it helps to really know the people you're working with. This year, I've spent time in Vancouver, Chicago, Hong Kong, and the UK because with the speed with which we've been doing some of the projects, being colocated with different vendors and different folks at times has been critical to getting things done more quickly.

Kimberly Wiessner

For cxpartners the start of the project is critical. They try to meet somewhere to kick off the project to make sure the team builds a strong relationship. At Experientia, a typical project team gets together several times during a project—at kickoff, at the end of field research. For them, the fluidity of in-person brainstorming and collaboration is important when they are transforming the research into design. Internal teams often got together at regular intervals to address their big issues. At a company where interaction designer Pabini Gabriel-Petit worked, they held quarterly get-togethers of a staff that was scattered around the United States and Canada. "It made sure we could get to know each other and settle strategic issues. Some people work well remotely, but others can't understand who you are unless they can see your face."

Another reason to travel is to get through a communications log-jam. Kevin Brooks described one project like that. A team in China had developed a new technology, but their documentation just didn't make sense to the people trying to use it. Messages weren't helping. This log-jam continued until one person went to China for 6 months. The length of time was important, as it was long enough to start to really work with the team in China, and not just be a guest. He became the go-between for the teams—a sort of cultural intermediary. Planning time with the team can prevent these sorts of communications problems. For any consulting or off-shoring project, it is important to have spent enough time with the main client team:

> It's important to be in the same room with the client, because that's the team. It's more efficient to produce the work when you are engaging with each other on a regular basis, and not waiting for time differences and calls and connections that don't work and files that don't get downloaded and all the things that are between two people working in a remote location. You get the complete view of the project—the people and the users, and your vision becomes whole, instead of being piecemeal ... which is the typical problem for this offshoring.
>
> **Jhumkee Iyengar**

Another approach is to make sure that teams from different offices have opportunities to work together. Building personal relationships is one of the reasons he would send someone to work with a group at the head office. As a design manager in a large corporation, Dennis Kei Yip Poon sees this as a good way to bridge the cultural barriers. Trent Mankelow described how Optimal Usability has kept their two offices in Auckland and Wellington from growing apart. "It's really important to mix up the teams among their offices so they don't silo themselves. We do have slightly different cultures in the offices—it's made up of so many things: personalities in the offices, the type of work being done, the office environment itself—all sorts of things. Lately, we're being a lot more deliberate about going between the two offices to make sure that the goodness is spread. It is a constant challenge, but we want to make sure that the team perceives this as one company."

Distance Collaboration

Good collaboration doesn't happen by itself. Distance collaboration takes effort (and good technology). You have to smooth the edges around working remotely. The wide range of new communications technologies helps. Desktop video conferencing tools and groupware tools are common. Being able to see expressions (and hand gestures) helps, as does being on a system where you can easily share files or see physical objects. Text-based chat programs are also useful, but definitely not a substitute for phone calls.

> We also have a chat room on the Communicator, where we can chat everyday for 15 minutes. If anyone is having a problem, they can bring it up. Some of the people we worked with in China, I've never met them or ever seen their face, just heard their voice. Now I wish that we'd incorporated more video or Skype into the project. It makes relationships … better.
>
> **Jhilmil Jain**

Reactions to working with video presence systems, however, varied. These systems are designed to make it seem as though the group is sitting around a single table. The video images and audio are much more realistic than earlier video conferencing systems. Some teams use them well, and are impressed with how fluid the good systems feel. But they work best for meetings. Workshop activities break down over distance, even with good video conferencing. In a group, you can't see expressions well, and the voice quality isn't good. It can also be difficult if the group is using physical objects like prototypes or Agile story cards.

Making distance collaboration fluid can be hard, but when you are the link between teams in two countries, Jhumkee Iyengar says, "you have to make communication an ongoing thing, perhaps picking up the phone twice a day. You have to make sure that what is happening in India stays in line with what the user needs." Setting a schedule, so that time to work together is built into your day is another way to ensure that you can make distance collaboration a priority.

> It worked the best when we started out co-located and spent three weeks working together. We could learn idiosyncrasies, and what we were each better at, so we could divide the work in a way that made sense. And then we spent a lot of time e-mailing files back and forth. We set up an hour at the end of every day to do a catch up and mini design critique. It let us review the designs we'd done for the day and talk about what we could have done better. That fed back into the work process the next day. It was a high bandwidth solution, but it worked very well. Throughout the day, we'd ping each other on IM, but we kept dedicated time to catch up. Our teams respected that time.
>
> **Darci Dutcher**

Supporting Collaboration and Innovation

Whatever physical relationships and communications tools you use, the goal has to be for the team to work together well. These days that means more than just productivity. A good team is both collaborative and innovative.

Global Teams and Diversity

One value of global teams is their diversity. The stories from the interviews echo the business management literature: diverse global teams that can tap the pool of global talent and provide a competitive advantage. When business researchers examined the advantages and disadvantages of virtual global teams and how well they functioned, they concluded that having a more heterogenous group made the team "more powerful and effective" than "traditional team structures influenced by time and place." In other words, all the work of building a global team pays off. (Bergiel, Bergiel, Balsmeier 2008)

THE U-SHAPED RELATIONSHIP BETWEEN DIVERSITY AND CULTURE

In their research of *transnational* teams, Earley and Mosakowski (2000) concluded that there is a U-shaped relationship between diversity and effectiveness.

- At one end of the U, traditional teams, made up of people from a single country, formed a unified team identity easily.

- In the middle, teams with low diversity, such as a team with one dominant group and a few people from other countries, formed subgroups and internal factions easily. These teams were the least effective.
- At the other end of the U, highly diverse teams with many cultures represented also worked well.

As Kevin Lee put it, "Some of the challenges are pretty obvious: Start with different cultural backgrounds and the fact that everyone brings in very different perspectives on a problem that you are trying to solve together. I think that's an obvious difficulty and challenge, but it's also opportunity to create and share understanding of what you are trying to accomplish at a global level, and therefore try to drive local products out of global level product development."

Cross-Cultural Communication

Although diverse teams bring value, the work of building a team is just a little bit harder. Cross-cultural communication demands an extra level of awareness. There are all the little adaptations to develop a communication style, all the small details of business etiquette and differences across cultures. Do you shout at someone across the room, or do you stand up and walk over to them? How do I know when I can talk to someone, and when they can talk to me? Being aware of these issues, but not obsessed about them makes a difference. Doug Wang said, "When you start working in a new office, you just expect that it will be different and that you will have to spend some time getting used to how they work."

That doesn't mean there is not culture shock. On one project, Darci Dutcher spent six months in India handing over a project to the team in Hyderabad.

> That was quite a culture shock. At the end of each session to go over a part of the project, I'd ask if they understand, and they'd say, 'Yes, yes it's fine.' A few days into this training, I asked someone to do something we had just talked about. They said, 'We don't know how to do that.' I was a bit perplexed. Eventually, I found out that they didn't want to ask questions because they thought I would be offended, thinking they meant that I had done a poor job on the training. At that point, I changed my approach, and just started working with them one-on-one.
>
> There were other cultural issues, too. I learned that most of my colleagues came from a culture within India where they had

been taught not to talk to women they weren't related to. And here's this loud-mouth California woman showing up and trying to talk to them. We got the issues worked out by the end with a level of comfort for everyone, but it took a little bit of work.

Darci Dutcher

Even within a single large team, different offices can develop different ways of working. These might be influenced by national cultures, but might also be a function of many other factors. Doug Wang suggests that, "People have to be adaptive to different ways of working. There is no standard because we are working with people (not systems). Each project might have a different way of working, depending on who is the leader. For example, if the project is being driven by someone in San Francisco, he would want his way of working together. Ditto a project led from Europe or Shanghai. The sweet point is in coming together and know we are all working together for a big team."

The lesson of these stories is that you have to listen carefully and take the time to find a communication and collaboration style that works for everyone.

Making Everyone Part of the Conversation

One of the roles of a manager is to act as a facilitator for the team, building relationships and ensuring that everyone is heard. This often starts with building social relationships and maintaining them. One practice is to start regular team meetings with 15 minutes of talk about personal things, just to know what's going on in each other's lives before going on to the business agenda.

Cultural differences in communication style can affect how well the team works. When power relationships or differences in perceived importance and seniority reduce the willingness of one group to speak openly (especially in off-shoring relationships), this is called the "mum effect" (Sajeev, Raminwong 2010). Cultural differences increase the risk, but one study that compared communication styles showed that professionals with longer experience in the workplace showed less tendency to be affected by this problem, suggesting that work environments can overcome issues in the general cultural environment.

Studies of collaboration stress the importance of the team dynamic. A study of student designers with a diverse team looked at how the team made sense of different aspects of a design problem (Larsson 2003). They concluded that it's important to view collaborative work as a social activity, not just an engineering or business process. For a team to come up with shared concepts, they have to be able to "think together," not just exchange information and opinions.

Workspaces that Support Collaboration

Many teams have rich workspaces that allow teams to be immersed in artifacts of their work. Marketing companies have a long tradition of creating *product rooms*, but this practice is getting more common in UX companies. At Optimal Usability, Trent Mankelow said they arrange (and rearrange) their offices to create a space that nurtures creativity. "We have a way to go to maximize our space, but we're thinking about things like the locations of white boards, and making pods of desks that face each other instead of everyone staring out the window."

People as Cultural Bridges

Another way that teams come together is through individuals who can act as a bridge between different cultural groups. Cultural bridges can be collaborators, adding details and insights about deep-rooted issues. Or, just like a local "buddy" can act as a guide in your first experience in a new culture, these people smooth out communication between different groups on a team.

> One of my projects involved working between two different functions in the company, one in Hong Kong and the other in New York City. Two people on the project were very tied into both locations. The first ran the software group. He was born in Hong Kong, went to Hawaii in his teens, went to college in the US, and then went back to Hong Kong. He was completely fluent in English, completely fluent in Chinese, and really functioned as a bridge between us.

> Another important bridge was a woman who worked in the Hong Kong office who really stood out. If you walked into a room filled with the people who worked in this office, she was the only one whose hair was dyed punk rock purple; right? She spoke fluent English—strong accent but fluent English—a mile a minute. She was a bridge to the day-to-day staff for us. She could hang out with the Americans and she had almost a salty kind of American humor, but she could also just walk into the Hong Kong office and speak the local language like they were day-to-day colleagues.

> The thing about these people is that they were not part of the mainstream in either Hong Kong or the US. They were both

cultural outliers in this context. That helped them be a bridge between the two groups.

Josh Seiden

When she works with research teams from the West making their first trips to China, Jo Wong often acts as a cultural bridge for teams making their first trip to China. "I try to think about it from their point of view. If I didn't know much about Chinese culture, what would be interesting? I may share perspectives from the news or other articles, but mostly I try to be myself and let people see Chinese culture through me." This part of her work is just as important as conducting the research interviews as she helps a team learn about a cultural context that is new for them.

LISTER AND MATTEO: CULTURAL CONNECTORS

Our team of designers on the ground in Zambia discover that meaningful connections and conversations can be as valuable as days of field work.

Undoubtedly, Lister and Matteo were two of the most important people on our trip. Matteo will be remembered for pulling the car under a tree while we went off to do our work, turning on the radio, opening the doors, and hosting an impromptu dance marathon with village children.

Lister not only navigated some pretty treacherous terrain with finesse and safety, but also enabled us to connect with some key individuals by acting as a translator and social bridge between Bemba-speaking Zambians and us. She found opportunities to fill those gaps, taking time to explain things to us and immerse us in the culture. This included helping us negotiate prices for fabric yardage (our most treasured trip souvenir), reminding us to bring toilet paper into our pit latrine adventures, and pulling over to buy about 5 lbs of dried caterpillars on the side of the road. (To her amusement, we did not partake.)

We were reminded that if you are open to it, you can learn as much from insightful people like Lister as you can through days of fielding. More than that, she might have been our most powerful in-field synthesis tool. A sounding board for questions, validations, curiosities, and stories. There's not much better than having multiple observations tied together in an understandable way by someone native to the culture.

Kate Calanes and Lauren Serota, Frog Design

You can read more about this research at the Frog Design blog, http://designmind. frogdesign.com/blog/ (Canales, Serota 2010).

Building UX and Cross-Cultural Knowledge

There is one final challenge for any team: how to keep the team's UX and cross-cultural knowledge and skills growing, even in the midst of busy project schedules. Bill DeRouchey points out that "A company has to be very intentional about spreading knowledge across projects and communicating that to the team and also to everybody else in the company that's not even on the project at all." Two forms of knowledge are important:

- General UX knowledge—Keeping fresh as a professional and staying up-to-date with the field, including approaches and techniques for global UX.
- Knowledge about different users, cultures, and markets—Sharing insights and information across a team, including people who may not have had direct contact with users.

Keeping UX Knowledge Fresh

Staying up-to-date with trends and techniques is a general concern for many of the people we interviewed. For managers, it's both part of maintaining a competitive edge and a way to attract and keep staff. For individuals, it's something they simply consider part of being a good professional. It's important for global UX because of the challenges working across geography and culture adds to any design or user research.

For some teams, integrating their UX knowledge into their daily work ideas included:

- Starting the day with a stand-up SCRUM-style meeting where each person can not only report on what they are working on, but also ask for input from others.
- Holding frequent critiques of work-in-progress and brainstorming sessions that allow people to pitch in ideas on any project.
- Running regular meetings that focus on developing UX knowledge, discuss different research techniques they have heard or read about, and think about how they can be used on projects.
- Internal workshops or "away days," which are other ways of setting aside time to talk about new ideas and share thinking on new directions for their work processes.

These techniques are part of a critical examination of any UX work, but are effective ways to also share cross-cultural knowledge.

Local Community

The local community is another source for knowledge building. Formal meetings, online communities, and informal meet-ups are all opportunities to hear new ideas or solutions to common problems. When there is no UX team, the local community may be even more important as a way to get feedback from peers and getting exposure to new ideas. You can use this to build relationships that can extend to day-to-day work.

The local community can also be a source of strength for teams in places far from major centers. In San Francisco, London, Bangalore, or Shanghai, it's easy to find presentations and meetings that bring input from around the world. But in more geographically isolated places, it can be hard to get a clear picture of how local work compares to the work from the global UX community. When Daniel teaches workshops he sometimes notices that very smart people lack confidence. As Raven Chai put it, "UX is still in infancy in Singapore, so it's still local variations on international best practices. But I don't think what we evolve here will be accepted as best practice by the global community."

Global Community

The global UX community is very much an online community. Most of the interviews for this book were conducted using Skype (complete with gaps where the call was dropped and had to be reconnected), based on introductions made through e-mail, Twitter, Facebook, and other networks, after conversations at work and at social and professional events. Despite all these ways to connect, face-to-face opportunities are still valuable.

Conferences are one way of staying connected to the broader UX community. They are an opportunity to hear new ideas as well as sharing your own. As Giles Colborne pointed out, one value of giving a talk is that it "forces you to think carefully about what you have learned and what you see as important for others."

In addition to the obvious benefits of the presentations and networking opportunities, conferences can offer opportunities to travel to new places. Trent Mankelow challenges his staff to use any travel as a chance to observe other cultures and visit other UX companies to learn about how they work. As he put it, "Even a simple thing like renting a car can be an opportunity to notice the process and interaction details more consciously. When you've been living in a house for a while, you don't notice the squeaky doors."

Global, Cultural Knowledge

Despite the emphasis on keeping up with UX knowledge, there are few groups that look for formal ways to capture cultural knowledge beyond the original project, even when they acknowledge that it could be part of creating a richer global picture across the company. One example is the team Hsin Eu leads at Trend Micro. They take a more formal approach: they collecting input from user research, customer service, marketing, and other sources and cataloguing it for future use.

Others wanted to have a robust way of consolidating this knowledge, but had not been able to find the resources to do so. Instead, they rely on sharing anecdotal information in casual conversations and on their institutional memory to keep track of resources.

> I would say we're in the messy category in terms of sharing feedback from customers or insights from research. We all have bits and pieces, understanding of different things, but generally we have folks concentrated around a specific project. The group that is focused on that project really gets immersed in that customer experience and what we are trying to accomplish. That gets shared out across the team in the form of formal reports generated after we do research. That said, a big piece of my job is taking what we're learning on each project and translating it into documentation that can be shared with teams all over the world.
>
> **Kimberly Wiessner**

Sometimes an individual will make it their mission to share their passion for their culture with their team. Doug Wang tries to build his view of Chinese culture into his own design principles, making them visible for his team and Wei Ding goes out of her way to share Chinese history and culture with their colleagues. She lives and works in the United States and realizes that many of the people in her company had never learned much about China's history. She does internal presentations for them, and says that she "feels privileged to be able to help bring the US and China perspectives together. It's a little outside my daily responsibilities, but I have a passion for it." She feels that a better understanding would help people in her company understand, for example, why the Chinese government reacts to things in a certain way.

RESEARCH IN THE FIELD

IN THIS CHAPTER

Devya is busy assembling photos to brief a team before they leave for home visits in Chennai. Xiang is conducting an interview in Guangzhou with his colleagues from Germany. Andre is on his way to Argentina for usability testing, and checking his Spanish vocabulary lists. Steve is sleepy as he listens to the simultaneous translation of a session being beamed to him from Singapore.

Running a successful global research project is not really that different from running any research project, except that the global nature of the project adds an extra layer of issues to the work of planning and managing the project. That makes the work exciting, but also a bit riskier and a little bit more difficult.

Whether the idea of research itself is new, or just the global aspect of research is new, "thinking globally" changes our ways of thinking about our markets, customers, and users. This change starts with your reasons to do global research at all: what perspectives and cultures you need to learn about.

You may have access to global teams, or a wider network for internal coordination. Working in many countries can mean collaborating with new local partners. Working in more than one language requires simultaneous interpreters or research staff who speak those languages. And, there are facts of business life. Projects can take longer and cost more. There's justifying the extra costs of international travel or the challenges of crossing traditional boundaries inside the corporate structure.

Some of the ways of dealing with the complexity of global work involve tactical adjustments. Others are approaches that extend practices in new ways.

In this chapter, we'll see how people currently working on global projects answer these questions:

- What are my goals for this research and how can I meet them?
- How do I plan and run a successful global research project?
- What UX research techniques are the best to use?
- Who should be part of a global research team?
- What preparation gets me ready for research in a new culture?
- How do I make the most of our time in the field?
- How do I work most effectively with global participants?

Setting Research Goals

Any research project starts by answering the question, "What are you trying to learn?" If that sounds obvious, it's because it's easy for a global research project to sound like open-ended fishing expeditions. You can't just "go see what people in China think." And you are certainly not going to understand everything about every person in India in a single visit.

Global Research Goals

Projects often have goals in several different time frames, from immediate design decisions to looking for strategic directions. For example, when Jhilmil Jain's company wanted to expand a product for the educational market into Brazil and Asia, the project—from initial planning through their feedback reports—took almost a year, much longer than a single local project. To make sure the results would be useful across this longer time frame, they had three sets of goals, with clear time frames for how each set of findings would be used:

- Immediate: What functional or aesthetic changes should they make?
- Short term: What are the needs of the teachers, parents, educators from an education point of view, and how are they different in those countries compared to their current markets?
- Three to five years: What are new technologies that we could develop for these markets and add to the product pipeline?

Sometimes the reasons to do research globally are just the same as the reasons to do any research: to have the data to make confident decisions.

> In my company, customer research ends all opinions, arguments, bickering about this or that. Going up to the owners of a product or business unit and telling them that customers give us feedback that they are confused by something usually means that the business will really take that to heart, and go back and reevaluate. Within the last couple of years, getting that customer's voice pulled back in through research has become immensely important. It's the thing that ends all opinionated arguments. The voice of the customer sets the direction of the vision for what we're going to do.
>
> **Kimberly Wiessner**

For every project, you have to ask, "What is the value of including participants from different cultures? What makes this project global?" rather than just being global for the sake of ticking a box on a list of research goals.

You might start by thinking about what aspects of your products create relevant differences across countries and cultures. For example:

- Is it affected by financial practices, such as habits for online payments, use of credit cards, or the structure of the banking system?
- Does it rely on social conventions and cultural norms, such as dating, entertainment, or family organization?
- Are the types of technology in use, such as computers, telecommunications, or household appliances, important in your industry?

You might want to plan your research locations around organizational needs. In planning research locations for PayPal, Jim Hudson looks at the product portfolios and the size of the markets, but also at how to include the widest possible cultural variation. "If we went to the US, the UK, and Australia, we might have covered a broad geographical area, but those three countries share a language and some cultural basis. They also have broadly similar methods of payment. So I might look for locations with not only different cultures, but also different attitudes and methods of payment."

Time in the Field

Next, you have to decide how you will meet your goals for global research, and how much time you will spend in the field. Many people we spoke with stressed the importance of getting out of the lab. As Joe Leech put it, "Getting someone into the lab can get you 70 to 80 percent of the way. You may find the usability answers, but not the cultural issues. You need the extra level of research to get the most out of situation." This is especially true if you are working in a culture that is new to you.

As much as you may want to spend a lot of time in the field this simply may not be possible. In global UX research, you must find a way to balance between the immersive techniques that produce the deepest insights and remote techniques that offer ways to extend the geographical research of your research without the difficulties and expense of travel.

Planning a Global Research Project

Like many things in this book, planning for global research takes you back to basics, like where and when to conduct the research, how many participants, and the project schedule.

When, and Why, to Travel

To UX people, the need is very clear: "You can't understand the user without understanding the eco-system around them," as Anjali Kelkar put it. That means getting out of the office and going to where the users are. If your responsibilities cover more than one local area, you have to travel to understand what colleagues, customers, and users are thinking.

Getting approval to travel is often a case of research goals meeting business realities. The decision needs to be based on what you want to learn, and whether it's possible to use technology to bridge the gap. Sometimes it isn't. Despite all the technologies, from telepresence to Skype, you can't replace physical presence completely for research or work within the team.

> If the question is, "Who are our users? Who do they interact with? What do they do?" then I would probably not settle for a phone interview or a screen sharing remote evaluations of some kind.

I would need to go there. And if there is enough "weight" in an area, for example, if we have a large user or customer population in two countries that are close to each other, then I would probably go there for a study. At Google if there is a good reason to run a study and there is travel needed, we go. If it's needed, it's needed, and there are no questions asked. And so I guess that really helps. It makes your life easier. But it hasn't always been like that. I remember in previous companies arguing that Israelis or Americans are not very representative of our user population, and all I got were nods and budget reasons for not going anywhere.

Tomer Sharon

Schedule and Number of Participants

Whether we like it or not, fast-paced projects are a fact of life. Companies can be impatient with primary research. For those who rely on design research, like Henning Fischer, this can be frustrating. "I'd like to stretch it out longer, but you have to get stuff done. Clients want to see insight immediately, and they want it to be actionable."

Costs are also an important consideration. Trips get scheduled to make the most efficient use of travel time, for example, by visiting several sites at each stop.

Whether the problem is the cost or the project schedule, the result can be schedules that seem to be more about being able to "tick the box" than doing good research. As Daniel put it, "we are starting to get increasingly annoyed at companies that are just playing the numbers game. They do this either through trying to cram too many sessions in a day because it's more cost effective, or they're trying to hit particular numbers of participants. They're not thinking through the quality of the research. They're not thinking about care for the people that are involved. There are all these run-on effects that organizations forget about, like how it will impact participants if the moderator is tired."

Some research cultures have always emphasized numbers, and how many participants you need to have confidence in your conclusions. This question is just as important in global research. Perhaps more so when a project that draws sweeping conclusions about the characteristics of a location or culture may be your only chance in a particular location. Global research, especially, asks you to be able to responsibly recount to those unfamiliar with this setting.

If you go out and do 30 in-home interviews, you're going to want to die by the end, because you have just packed in so many meetings without time to think through what you have learned. I honestly believe that if you meet with 12 people and engage with emotional intelligence, your findings are going to have more of an impact and you're going to get to something much deeper and a much better understanding. You have to come back and be able to retell those stories. If your enthusiasm and energy is gone and you're emotionally depleted, you're not going to be able to do that research justice. It's really about scoping your work in such a way that no only do you know you can go out and get the research, but you can deliver it back. This is something I've really had to come to terms with in my own work.

Rachel Hinman

Time for Local Logistics

One factor that makes global projects hard is dealing with the practical arrangements for the research in many different locations. Jhumkee Iyengar remembered a project that ended with an Indian company dealing with an irate client from the West. "Against their better judgement about the local environment, they packed in too tight a schedule. It was in a large city, with long, unpredictable travel between locations. In the local culture, unpunctuality is taken in stride, with no expectation for keeping to precise times. Normally they would build the schedule to allow for this. When they could not keep to the unrealistic schedule set, everyone was upset."

You may also need to adjust expectations about how a session runs. Although some cultures expect efficiency and to just dive into the questions, others include time for socialization even in simple exchanges. Offering tea and cookies to participants may be part of basic hospitality, even in a business setting, not an interruption in the work day.

Time for Analysis

No matter how and where you run a research project, you need to plan how you will do the analysis, especially if you are combining work from several different places.

If you have one team traveling to many places, think ahead to how you will compare your observations from one place to another. If you are coordinating the work of many teams, you may have people in different countries all bringing their own perspectives and methods.

In her mobile Internet study for Nokia, Anne Kaikkonen found that they had to be careful that they were able to compare data collected in different countries. This included making sure that they compared the same types of sites.

You have to make sure that everybody understands the goal of the study in the same way, understands what is important and what you are looking for. If they don't, you won't be able compare the data that you gather to analyze the differences between the locations. The analysis is already challenging because people in different countries and different locations perceive things in different ways. In Asia the mobile Internet meant only web sites tailored for mobile use, whereas in Europe and the United States, people meant any web site you accessed through a phone or other device, even if it was the same one they used from their PC.

Anne Kaikkonen

Time for Discovery

When the question is big, you don't really want to confine it at first. Perhaps you are just starting a new project, or your company wants to learn more about a new market. You probably want to start with some kind of immersion, just to get to know the environment. Even if you don't have a full project for open-ended research, give yourself some time for what Bill DeRouchey calls "pure discovery." This is time you can spend just looking around to help you frame what the problem is. For example, one of his projects centered on sport: playing everyday and social sports. "We went to parks and playgrounds and sports fields to see how people play. You try to learn as much as you can around the world of sport. From there, you can narrow down the kind of activities you are interested in, to formulate an overall framework on how to think about the project." Notice that this is not aimless observation, but directed at spending a little bit of time learning about relevant activities. "If you have no scope to the research whatsoever, you might as well get an apartment and live in China for a year."

Choosing UX Techniques for Global Research

There are just as many choices of techniques in global research as in any other type of research. Most people started from their favorite techniques, modifying them as needed to fit the demands of global projects. At HSBC, Kim Wiessner emphasized the variety in their approach. "The types of user research we do can be just about everything you can imagine. Everything from a usability study toward the end of a process to more of a discovery or exploration study at the beginning of a process."

Given the wide variety of disciplines and types of projects represented in the interviews for this book, it's not surprising that both favorite techniques and the terminology used to describe them were equally varied. Joe Leech and many others commented that the same research techniques they use in any project work in global research as well, as long as they were willing to respond to an issues. "You can't be too dogmatic. You have to be able to adjust to the situation as it unfolds."

By far the largest number of people emphasized UX work early in a project. They called it design research, user research, and foundational research, but all were focused on learning about people in different environments in an open-ended way. For this work, everyone preferred techniques that allowed observation and open-ended interviews. "As the team that has to build the products, you have to understand the context. Nothing is better than going out and being able to shadow or talk to customers, understand how they use your products," Kevin Lee told us.

Some projects explicitly aimed to gather data for personas. Going to customer sites in different countries allowed Peter Grierson to gather data for robust personas. He used them to highlight differences in attitudes and business practices between customers in different countries, and gaps between how users view the product and how it is viewed internally.

For usability testing projects, whether testing an existing product or a prototype design in progress, there was a clear preference for using think-aloud or self-narrated tasks in an unstructured session. Giles Colborne emphasized that an experienced moderator has to be ready to follow the unexpected things that crop up, being flexible and responsive to the participant within the framework of the research goals.

Multiple Questions, Multiple Methods

It's common for there to be several related research questions, so many projects involve multiple methods.

> When I'm doing the research for product development, there are usually multiple questions. It is very common to have different methods in one single project. For example, if we are investigating how people are using mobile Internet, then we might have an online questionnaire, we may install an application that logs what people are doing. Then we can have interviews and observations and this kind of activity. Both qualitative and the quantitative data.
>
> **Anne Kaikkonen**

Research Techniques Framework

For her mobile UX research, Rachel Hinman thinks about the relationship of the researcher and the participant. She considers whether the researcher will be working directly with the participant or not, and then considers who much the researcher invades the participant's world, making them aware of the research. By choosing methods that includes techniques from at least two of the quadrants, the creates a research plan that allows her to look at a question from several different viewpoints.

"Whenever I formulate a research project, I always try to hit at least two if not three of those quadrants with the methods I choose. If you think of it, any type of research is kind of an intervention into someone's life.

"When the researcher is present and the participant is very aware, that is something like an in-home interview. You're there. You're present. You're altering the way in which they normally do things. If you are there and they know you are there,

it's obviously a very apparent intervention into their life and there's ways you have to negotiate that.

"What you miss in that sort of research, you can pick up through another method. For example, in a diary study the participant is very aware that they're doing research but you're not present. This lets you compare what that person said to you face to face, and what that person actually recorded in their diary.

"Finally, you might use a method where the participants are not aware of you at all. This might be for a project where traffic patterns—how people navigate a space—are very important. You may have cameras and you just watch people as they move through a space. This lets you think about that movement and the physical design of the space."

Rachel Hinman

You can see Rachel's presentation on Mobile UX Essentials on Slideshare at http://www.slideshare.net/Rachel_Hinman/mobile-ux-essentials-6643654.

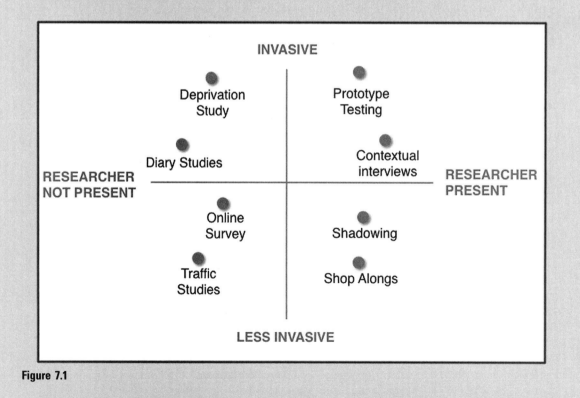

Figure 7.1

Users in Their Own Environment

Everyone wants to get out into the field and see users in context. This does not have to mean a full year of academic-style ethnography. We heard about many ways to do what some called "discount ethnography." They used the approach and methods in a more informal and more rapid project. This can be as simple as visiting homes or workplaces, or even just moving usability testing sessions out of the lab. It's not the amount of time you spend, but how well you take any opportunity to observe. Ideas for new ways of thinking can come from any source, even from small behaviors or details of the environment.

> On all of our design projects, we get out and try to experience the customer's product. Get into the call centers if they have them and listen to the staff. It could be visiting a store and just lurking. Or buying things and trying to exchange them. Discount ethnography is a great way to learn things that you don't get in the nice quiet calm environment. It's going to see people in their homes or offices and seeing how they really do it in the chaos of their own environment.
>
> **Giles Colborne**

Getting out into the field can also be important for people working with cutting edge technology. It's hard for people to understand and absorb a new idea in a short interaction in the lab. Describing her work testing speech and natural user interfaces, Jhilmil Jain says that, "first experiences tend to be very polarized. They either love it and totally get it or they don't get it at all. I'm in the process of designing a plan with field studies, and get feedback periodically, so we can track how perceptions and attitudes are changing over time."

People working in any market where their type of product is just being introduced faced similar problems. Don't think this always means moving technology from developed to emerging markets: Ideas move in all directions. Kevin Cheng says that when Tom Chi, his partner on the OK/Cancel comic, started working on Yahoo! Answers, the whole idea of a Q&A site was unknown in the West, but very popular in Taiwan. Their research focused on how to translate the underlying assumptions about how you participate on the Web to the culture in the United States. He says, "It's very rare that a company consciously picks up a trend that started in Asia, but there is a lot of borrowing that isn't really acknowledged, especially in games. As an example, virtual goods have been big in Asia for a long time, but only recently introduced in the US."

Other Research Sources

People who worked in larger companies often had several sources of information: market research, brand awareness research, market reports on activities relevant to their product, local partners doing targeted user research. For example, Wei Ding, who works for an international hotel chain, put together a portfolio of research that included information from both internal sources (channels used to make reservations and customer reviews), bespoke research (local research into expectations about hotels), and industry research (global internet behavior). This lets her keep up with the latest trends, and put all the information they need in one place. Similarly, the customer experience team at HSBC includes "a whole team that just looks after complaints, so we are really trying to understand where the customer issues are. We're circulating that up to the very top levels of the organization so the learnings can be addressed from the top down."

But Not Focus Groups

One thing everyone agreed on is that focus groups are not the answer. They preferred research that went deep into individual experiences, even if they could only do a few of them. Bill DeRouchey expressed it this way. "They don't really tend to be that effective in a lot ways because a lot of group think sets in. Focus groups typically take people out of their natural environment and into a facility with six other people they don't know and it creates almost a false atmosphere—not false but it creates an atmosphere that's not as conducive to getting to the truth of whatever the situation is."

Another challenge with focus groups, and any technique that takes people out of their natural environment, is that it also removes cues that keep them grounded in real life. On one project Anjali Kelkar researched use of cleaning products in the home. "You can't expect people to remember things with low involvement. Cleaning products are all low involvement things, so it helps to be in their place and see the whole process. Rigor in using processes and tools is important, but it can get in the way of understanding what people do spontaneously in their daily lives."

Although focus groups provide an opportunity for follow-up questions, they don't allow for the sort of unstructured one-on-one interview or bring objects from the immediate environment into the discussion.

We once interviewed a lady about her water use here in England. We asked her if she ever looked at the bill and whether it's clear to her. She said, "Yeah. I get one. It's clear. It's not very difficult, really." We asked her to actually show the bill and explain it to us. While explaining, it suddenly became clear that it's not clear at all. She doesn't actually understand at all what that bill is trying to tell her. That's really important to illustrate. The environment where you talk to people is crucial because if we hadn't been there, it would have been very difficult to achieve in a focus group setting.

Bas Raijmakers and Geke van Dijk

Remote Methods

Almost all of our research techniques can be modified in some way to work remotely. For example, screen sharing software makes it possible to look at a web site along with a participant. Of course, you are not *as present* as when you are there in person, but if you think carefully about the benefits and limitations, you can often get good results, even if you can't travel. For example, you can substitute diary studies for in-home visits, or use an online method for card sorting. Remote work is more difficult, however, for nontraditional computer devices, such a mobile phones or TV screens, where screen sharing tools are not available.

Most importantly, however, remote research and remote usability testing enables you to include more international participants, no matter where you are located. When IEEE made a commitment to usability testing for their web site, they also wanted to be sure that members from around the world were included. For them, having the global reach into an international membership can be more important than having the participant in the room. At Google, Tomer Sharon also uses remote techniques to keep his projects as global as his team. And many others use phone or Skype interviews with screen sharing to walk through daily work for her enterprise projects. On one project, Darci Dutcher asked people to use screen recording tools such as Silverback or Camtasia to record themselves as they use the prototype. Because they are in the same company, it's easy for the participants to post the video files to a server. New remote testing tools enable similar techniques.

Even if you are working directly with a participant, you may want to use tools for remote sessions to enable other team members to observe. Jhilmil Jain's lab enables remote viewing, so the entire team can participate. "We have a very collaborative environment, we all look out for each other. Even when we are

Tools for Remote Research
Bolt|Peters maintains a list of tools on their site, Remote Research: Tools, tips, and tirades about remote user research, at http://remoteresear.ch/tools/.

running usability testing here, I'll have people who will volunteer to take notes or observations. This might even be remote note-taking. The setup is nice: I can run a test in the lab and people anywhere can see the lab and take notes." Both Jhumkee Iyengar and Whitney have used these tools to observe usability tests being run by a partner, keeping them in touch with the research in a more immediate way than watching recordings. There's something about knowing that the session is going on *right now* that makes it more compelling.

Choosing the Team

The decision about who should travel for a project can be practical. For example, if there are people in the group who speak the language, or have experience somewhere, they can be an obvious choice. Managers have to consider work-life balance. Is the right person in a position to travel? Many UX companies, like Optimal Usability, have a young staff, many raising families. They are concerned with creating a balanced life, as well as doing great work.

But most look for people who have the right attitude for the work, are interested in the research location, and have a passion for discovery about other people and cultures. At User Vision, Chris Rourke found that if you can choose someone who is really keen on the idea of working somewhere, the passion they bring to the work and the challenge of experiencing another culture really pays off. "I would choose someone who says, 'Wow, I'd love to spend a few weeks out in the Middle East,' over someone who is not as interested in that experience."

> When I think about who I want to work with, curiosity is absolutely the top of the list. For me it's a strong indicator of a lot of other attributes. Some of the most successful designers and folks in this UX field are curious. They are insatiably curious about everything. They assume they don't have the answers. The assume that the way they are thinking about something isn't necessarily the only way.
>
> **Robert Barlow-Busch**

The skills are very basic. Team leaders start by looking for someone who knows the culture well or has some connection to it. After that, they look at a very short list of characteristics:

- Communication skills
- Observation skills
- Flexibility and adaptability

People Outside of UX

Many people talked about having non-UX people on the team. There's the obvious benefit of giving clients and business partners first-hand experience, but often there are more intangible benefits for how the work is received.

> If I can get the product manager to go on site with the research team, everything else is so much easier. It's always powerful when they can see things first hand, even more powerful for international research. They are stuck with you for the two to three days of testing. And between sessions. And a dinner. You end up having all these conversations and collaborative sense-making. You argue, and agree. The report just documents what we talked about, and we can now focus not on 'what happened' but on how to fix it. It makes my work easier and more productive.
>
> **Jim Hudson**

> No matter how many pictures or video there is always a little gap that the imagination can't fill. So, I always invite one partner from another department. When they come back to their own team, they can also tell the story with me. I think that's powerful as well. I may be the only researcher, but everyone can be part of the research, as long as they know how to respect the work.
>
> **Yu-Hsiu Li**

Being part of the team can also help change attitudes toward UX research. On one project, Anjali Kelkar had what she described as a very complicated team. It was cross functional, but also globally representative. The team had people from the United States, Mexico, Thailand, China, and India, all trying to understand what middle class in India is. It included people from Consumer Insights, R&D (in two countries), and a second research consultancy. It was a very challenging project to manage. One issue was the diversity of the team, but it was also a group of people used to thinking about quantitative data. It took time and a process to help them understand what they would learn from more qualitative methods.

Other teams include people from other departments within the project. When you take developers out to a customer site, it can become a turning point for the project. Peter Grierson described it as having personalized the research for the developers by showing them how their work played out in someone else's life. Having met some of the real people, the personas became living parts of the design process, not just aesthetic artifacts.

People from some of the most global companies made a strong case for having people from all parts of the product staff included in the research.

> When we put a team together, we might have representatives from engineering, research, design, product management, and management. We also want people from each office and people who are covering the country we are interested in, so they have a stake in the study. And, in the country where we do the research, we have some local people who will join us. I also wanted engineers who do not usually see clients join me so they will tell their friends what is going on with this market and with these users. So, you can see it has both a business, a global, and a political aspect for coming up with this team.
>
> **Tomer Sharon**

One way to not only include people from other departments is to add people from the local office who can be full cultural interpreters, helping you understand the entire context. You may have to teach them how to be part of user research, but the payoff in having them deeply involved is that you get people who understand the company's products as well as the local culture.

Researchers and designers may be part of one UX group, or may be in separate departments. Depending on the structure of your company or client, you may find designers automatically included or have to reach out to them. This variation is not limited to large companies. Some UX companies make it a strong point that their designers do their own research, rather than relying on a different group of people within their organization; others have specialized research groups.

> At Ziba, the designer is always on the project at the beginning. We don't divide the work up into researchers and designers. Instead, we ask the researchers and designers to think together: What is the framework for thinking about this project? What are the appropriate questions? What are the big research questions we are trying to answer? What is the core challenge? What is the essence? Of course, the researchers are more skilled at formulating those questions and framing them up in ways that can be tackled during the research process, and then formulating what that research process is, doing the actual interviewing, doing the actual synthesis of the data afterward. But we always include the designers in the field so they can see firsthand because we can avoid a level of translation in the handoff from researchers to

design. Some things don't have to be spelled out because they saw them together, experienced the same thing.

Bill DeRouchey

Not everyone agrees. For them, having professional researchers is more important because, they say, it takes trained skills to make the most of the opportunities. Sometimes we think that bringing the designers to the site visit or local visit will take care of the problems, but if not planned well, this can be a costly mistake. Kevin Lee points out that some people adapt well to research challenges and others don't. This comes back to finding people with the skills and interest to take advantage of the opportunities of global research. It comes back to being aware of yourself and your own cultural and historical perspectives.

What we act in a professional capacity, it is important to realize that we're observing and interpreting something through a mental filter—a filter that we may not even be aware is there. I think it's important ask ourselves what measures we can take to understand our own biases. Because getting out and experiencing new situation is going to be useful only if we are prepared to see things maybe in a new way.

Robert Barlow-Busch

Local Partners

The alternative to travel is to hire a local company to do the research. The advantage of this arrangement is not only the local knowledge that they bring, but the way that knowledge can enhance the project. Local partners can translate cultural issues, but can also suggest specific research questions appropriate to their location. You can deliberately choose partners for the value of their insights into a local environment, or to provide a contrast to your own team.

Because I was born and bred in Singapore I have inherited some concepts and ideas from our culture. The way to get around this is user research. On one project, we commissioned a Australian market research company. Their outside view helped give us a new perspective. They started from "ground zero" and started with a broad-based research, to validate assumptions. They found some surprises—for example, that local *heartlanders* were more receptive to new concepts than we had assumed. Their ability to bring us new perspectives shifted our thinking to a more positive view of working with a research partner.

Raven Chai

Companies may start with a single research partner, but as they get more experience, extend their pool of vendors and agencies to get a better understanding of the trends in the market. Another typical arrangement is that one person anchors the projects, traveling to all research locations, but with different partners in each place. The important thing is that you are able to build a relationship based on a similar outlook to the work. That sort of "meeting of the minds" makes it easier to work together.

The use of local partners can be a simple, practical, budget decision.

> Site visits are costly. They take a lot of time just for operations and logistics. Sometimes the enterprise doesn't appreciate their value. So, sometimes you use local service vendors or local individuals where you can create a partnership. The key, however, is to keep them involved so that their objective point of view of what was learned can be applied to informing product or experience decisions.
>
> **Kevin Lee**

Consulting companies working on global work may also rely on local partners to expand the reach of a small company. As Michele Visciòla from Experientia, a design firm based in Europe, put it, "I don't have any other way to do it. Projects cross borders, so they often need people in several countries." They hire people in countries where they have a project to work with the core design group in Italy. Their researchers go out to work with local people on the research, and then bring their understanding to the design team. This approach was typical of smaller design companies, no matter where they are based.

> We designed a web site for a German academic exchange program to encourage students worldwide to study in Germany. Before we designed anything we needed to find out what would motivate students to study in Germany, so we did research in six countries—India, Turkey, Brazil, China, USA, and Russia.
>
> It was great being able to rely on a global network of partner companies, because we needed to be able to trust our partners to deliver the information we needed to build a useful web site. We started fairly broad and narrowed things down to what really mattered over the course of the project, so there were lots of group calls and web conferences. It really helps if all partners are comfortable speaking with one another, so that you can do group calls instead of sequential one-on-ones.

It's really about being able to have a personal relationship with your local partners, and know their strengths and weaknesses, how to communicate, which terminology to use, and what to expect and not expect. This is even more important in an international context, because there is definitely more room for misunderstandings and cultural hiccups. Working with trusted partners should feel like working with your own team.

Jakob Biesterfeldt

Working with Local Offices Is Powerful

When Jhilmil Jain led a research project that spanned the United States, China, and Brazil, she used the local company offices to help her with local planning and running the research sessions. The product was for the educational market, so the local offices identified schools they could contact, helped them approach parents, and made sure that they understood local laws about working with children.

The team for each location included two UX researchers and two people from the local business unit. They spent a week together doing observations, interviews, and in-home visits. What started as a practical tactic—an easy way to get local logistical help and translation—turned into much more.

They trained the non-UX people to be part of the research, taking notes and running the video. "None of them had a lot of experience asking questions. Sometimes they would really mess up and ask a question in a way that really biased the users. We did a couple of pilots and could see this in advance. In-home was awkward the first time, but then they learned what to look for and what they can learn. When we did the in-home visits, we took a lot of product managers along with us. We (researchers) did the facilitating, but they could let us know what kinds of things they wanted answers for. It was just so powerful to have them along. It sold them the research."

In a company where the product teams really listen to the local sales office, when the local team was involved with the process, this made a difference to how the research was received. They were more enthusiastic about the findings. And that got buy-in from the product managers in the sales division.

Preparing for the Field

First, challenge your assumptions. Being open to experiences that challenge your assumptions is a recurring theme in global UX. It's especially important as you prepare to go into the field. We have all gathered at least a few assumptions from our own previous experiences. This is the time to bring them out into the open, so you can examine them, and be ready to change them. "For example, even if you have done research in a country before," Anne Kaikkonen points out, "things may have changed. Or I missed something in my earlier research and have built up a framework of ideas based on that misunderstanding."

Or, as Anjali Kelkar put it, "When you read that there's an 8.7% growth rate in India, you might think that Mumbai is like Shanghai. Good grief no. There is still a cow in the middle of the street, but your research participant's home might have six air conditioners. And possibly be equipped with every single appliance on the planet—all of which are state of the art."

Local Resources

When you sit down to inventory your own local resources, you might be surprised.

- Your own history might be useful. Do you have personal experiences from your home, university, or work?
- Maybe you know people from different cultures and can interview them.
- Books can be useful, especially for basic facts about the country or business etiquette

You may find that you have local resources, even if you don't think of your city as particularly global.

Pittsburgh (where Carnegie Mellon University is located) is a very international city. We have folks coming into these universities and hospitals from all over the world. So we can access any culture there is here. What I would do is look up those cultural groups here in Pittsburgh and go have conversations with them about how to handle these situations in that culture.

Jenna Date

Getting the Team Ready

If you are leading the team, think about what each person needs to do to prepare. Some may be skilled researchers, but need a background in the culture; others may come from the research location, but have never been part of UX research.

One challenge for our projects is that with such a big team, making sure that everyone understands why we are going, what we're going to do there exactly. Some of them have never been exposed to research at all. Another challenge is to make sure that everyone behaves during the sessions. We are going to visit clients at their offices. This is not a trivial thing for these clients. Having three foreigners come and watch you while you work is not an easy thing. We are going to go through some cultural training sessions to make sure that we know what we need to know about the expected behavior of both us and the participants.

Tomer Sharon

Ultimately, you want to make sure that everyone is on the same page before you start the research sessions. Good preparation can make things go more smoothly when everyone understands who you will be working with, why they were selected, and what you hope to learn.

Preresearch: Preparing the Team

Before going into the field, Anjali Kelkar says it's important to get the team ready. "It is critical to do this work before we start the actual field work. Getting all the questions and assumptions out lets us get on the same page and get down to work." The preresearch process starts with a reading list to help the team learn about the country and culture. At the research location a small number of participants do a diary study around issues relating to the research questions.

Then, there is a one-day workshop with the entire team. This is not just the people who will actually go on the research trip, but everyone from the front desk staff to the directors. The goal is to let everyone share the same data, gather their impressions before the research, and go through the previsit research including the diaries, demographic data, and stock photos collected for the project.

One exercise is the Assumption Breaker. "People are allowed to be their most judgmental, and say the most horrible things they have in their mind. Anything and everything they have in their mind. No holds barred. They've heard *something* about that culture all their life and they just can't let go of what they think they know." All of these statements are collected on sticky notes, so they are visible. Then the team starts to break down their own assumptions and get at the reality behind them. "What I want people to see is that they *have* these assumptions. Some are right, some are not. When we pull out the pictures from people's homes—real photos from real homes—it starts breaking down a lot of the assumptions, as well as validating and modifying some."

When the team gets to the site, they start with immersion "soak-ins" on first landing. "Streets, shopping malls, different kinds of stores. What's it like at night. A cultural ride through the areas you are going to visit. This is getting people sort of familiarized with what they might encounter, with photographs in front of them and local people who can answer questions. It's instant and immediate. It's rapid immersion."

You can learn more about Anjali's research approach from a talk recorded at the IIT Design Research Conference 2010, at http://vimeo.com/12370143.

Being in the Field

As we look at what it's like to be in the field, we'll focus on two challenges: exhaustion (both mental and physical) and language.

Research is hard work at the best of times. Add the overhead of working across time zones and cultures, in a different language, and with projects that often have high expectations, and the cognitive overhead can be exhausting. One reason is that we spend a lot of time empathizing with people and situations that may be very different from our own lives, so that we can understand them.

> Research can be really emotionally draining. When I was doing research about diabetes, it was hard research for me to do because we were meeting person after person who was diagnosed with a really difficult illness. You had to get to know that person and how the disease affected their life. When I was in Uganda, I spoke with a lot of women there. My heart really went out to them and some of the challenges they have to face on a daily basis. There's a balance between allowing yourself to be open but also giving yourself the kind of time and space to process the information and honestly, when you're in the field, take care of yourself and keep everything in balance.
>
> **Rachel Hinman**

Pace Yourself

One challenge for long-haul research is making it manageable for the human beings who are doing it. Perhaps one reason these projects are often so memorable is that they tend to be both high profile and hard work. But global research should not be thought of as a once-in-a-career experience, but something that is part of your normal work. You may have to reduce the number of people you work with in a day, or give yourself time between interviews to absorb what you have learned.

> In one project, we did 13 straight days of interviews, two to three interviews a day, in the UK, France, and Germany. At the end of it, we were completely wiped out. Completely. Just managing your endurance is absolutely critical. Not only are you doing research, which is hard enough by itself, but you are doing it in an environment, one that you are disoriented in most of the time. There's a massive cognitive overhead that goes along with it. Recognizing that and planning for it is part of the work. I do this by lowering my expectations of what might be possible in a fixed time frame.

It's easy to do three interviews a day for five days in the US, because I know the US, but in Japan it's a whole different thing. You have no idea what's going on around you. You have no idea where you are. The language barrier is absolute, so you rely on your local guide. Fortunately, everywhere we've gone our local guides have been great, but you are still relying on one person. If there's any hint that they are not on top of things or that things are not going perfectly, it makes you wonder. You are on a tight schedule, and this is costing someone an awful lot.

Henning Fischer

People have to find ways to protect themselves. Henning suggests a tactic echoed by several other people. "Even just shutting down in your own hotel room. That's a thing that I do when I'm feeling overwhelmed. Or, I might also just go for a walk with my iPod on. It's really fun in Japan because you get a soundtrack to something that's entirely alien to me. I went around the Imperial Palace listening to The Who."

Other Experiences

Getting out of "the lab" isn't just a good tactic to keep your perspective. It's also a way to build your sense of the location and culture. You can just take in the local environment, as Yu-Hsiu Li does when he travels. "I like to listen to their radio, and watch their TV, and even go talk to street vendors to try to understand their perspectives and what is popular. It's more about the experience of their life. That's how you can share their experience." He's not talking about going half-way around the world here, just crossing into China from Taiwan.

Or you can add activities like watching a sports game, visiting interesting parts of town, just going to a grocery story, or sitting in a cafe watching daily life. With all the things you have to do on a trip, it's easy to forget socializing with the team to build bonds around the shared experience.

The visits always involved a lot of socializing. The Hong Kong team was very, very generous with their time as hosts. We spent a lot of time with them. The New York team spent a lot of time together on the Hong Kong visits. So the New York team became very close because of all of that travel. You feel like you are going through a shared experience that forges a bond. We traveled well on that project. There was a lot of camaraderie developed on those trips. We were able to build real relationships, that helped make the whole project go better.

Josh Seiden

Working Effectively with Participants

You have to come to the research ready to engage—if you aren't emotionally and physically ready to be there, you don't get much of value from the session. But then you have to relax and be patient. Give yourself a license to take the time to dig deeper. After all, the whole point of global UX research is to understand people from cultures different than your own. You need to do more than fire questions at people. Your facilitation techniques need to create a space where you can meet them on their terms. That's a very different attitude from feeling you always have to be in control.

> Whenever I've walked away from an interview and felt that it went really well, it was this really great subtle dance of a person sort of telling me really relevant information but also creating the context where they felt really comfortable doing so. I think it's a real skill to be able to create a place where people feel really comfortable talking about themselves and telling you their opinions about things as you gently guide the conversation. It's a matter of picking up on threads, being patient, and giving them time to say the things that sometimes may not seem relevant. But also knowing when to go deeply into an idea. Some people really have a talent for it, but I think it's also just a skill that you have to develop with experience.
>
> **Rachel Hinman**

It's also important to take the time to build trust between your team and the participant, one of the values of the preresearch that Anjali Kelkar asks participants to do. "I start with the photos the user has taken for you of their daily lives. So, in a way, they have already brought you into their home before you even ring the doorbell. This acts as an icebreaker, because it means there is already empathy between your research participants and your team." She also finds that the visuals can improve the discussion. "You can't just ask someone a question and expect it to trigger a story. We need the pictures taken by the participants about their lives to start the story. That's when I start saying, Can you tell me more about these pictures? Which is your favorite picture, why?' And as they start describing their life through the pictures and point to various things, I ask, oh, can you show me? and we start moving around the house looking at things."

Bas Raijmakers and Geke van Dijk go even farther, working directly with their participants to make films that represent their experience. The films are made in such a way that the viewer can identify with the person—step in their shoes and take the

Let *Them* Teach *You*
This is the essence of ethnography. Instead of collecting "data" about people, the ethnographer seeks to learn from people, to be taught by them. ... In order to discover the hidden principles of another way of life, the researchers must become a *student*. Spradley - The Ethnographic Interview (1979)

perspective of the participants for a little time. Sometimes they invite the research participants to a session with the team, so that there is also an encounter between people.

Another way to allow participants to take their time is to leave time at the end of the session for a general conversation. Although many researchers might not think of allowing the observers to talk directly with participants, Ding Wei described the value of this in one global project. "They said things they probably wouldn't have said in the recorded part of the session. That was amazing. I still remember some of the quotes."

Recruiting

It's easy to think of finding participants as just a preliminary requirement, but, recruiting is part of the research. Like everything else in global research there are special challenges.

First, you may not be able to easily define the people you want to work with. "Clients start with an idea—their picture of their customers. This tends to be a profile based on their marketing concepts," says Michele Visciòla, "but they are doing this research to discover or refine their marketing concepts, so they don't have an accurate profile yet."

Second, because you are working across cultures, language, and nationality, you may have to redefine your screening requirements. The same questions that work in one country may not work in another one, no matter where you start from. This might be as simple as knowing how to define income brackets, or how to ask questions about daily life. In Hong Kong, for example, the question isn't whether someone has a mobile phone, but how many they have and how recently they got a new one. Another example is that in US Latino families, using the Web is often a social activity within a family. Younger family members, with more exposure to technology often help their parents and relatives by finding information for them. Simply asking, "Do you use the Web?" might not get you the participants you expect.

Finally, you need to make sure that you and the participants both understand what will happen.

- Think about how to explain what you want them to do. In some countries, people will not commit until they understand who you are and what you are asking of them.
- Make sure you understand how the people you want to work with think about time. Are they likely to be prompt or loose about schedules? Will they make a commitment in advance, or do you need to recruit very close to the times when you want to work with them?

- In cultures that are not as comfortable sharing or speaking about themselves, think in advance about how you could motivate them. It may be as simple as saying that you are there to learn from them.

Language Matters

The other big issue for global UX research is language. Even if you speak the language well enough for normal conversation, there are local nuances of language to consider.

> You have to weigh the pros and cons of running your own sessions. If you are speaking in a second language, do you know it well enough to work effectively? I've had some great rapport with people when I've been in South America, just me speaking my not so perfect Spanish. I think there's more likelihood that a local moderator will be able to establish that rapport better than a foreign moderator. However, a fairly proficient test moderator may also be able to make those connections, because this is a basic moderation skill. There are limits. Trying to moderate eight people speaking Spanish, voicing their opinions in their own natural language, their own subtleties of words and things, I definitely couldn't handle that. In that kind of case, I would definitely want to have a native Spanish speaker handle a focus group.
>
> **Chris Rourke**

One risk is not knowing local idiom or slang. Taking notes for her first usability test in the United Kingdom, Whitney was pretty confident. After all, she spoke native English. Until a participant announced in a firm, but neutral voice that she was "really chuffed" about a change the organization had made recently. Was that good or bad? Luckily, the next sentence clarified the point. It was a good reminder that there are variations in any language, and English (US) is not the same as English (UK). When you have to stop and ask for an explanation, it breaks the flow of the interview.

Having someone local conduct the session solves this problem. This might be a interpreter, but UX researchers often work with a partner agency or a freelancer who can both translate the language *and* the culture, helping you understand what people actually mean and how to interpret their behavior. Even if you do your own research, local people expand your viewpoints. An additional advantage for the research is that they add people to the team who may bring a different perspective and a different view of the world.

Your own (or your moderator's) accent can be a problem as well, especially if several different languages are involved. How

Culture in Usability Testing

Does the culture of the usability moderator matter? One research project found that participants found more usability problems and made more suggestions when the moderator was from the same culture. It only took a small reference to culture to create this effect. Ravi Vatrapu and Manuel Pérez-Quiñones, (2006) acceptable an accent is depends a lot on the specific context and the comfort level of the client or the participants. Samir Chabukswar found that an accent that was OK in California caused problems in other areas of the United States. But the bottom line is that the participants have to be able to easily understand the questions and interact as naturally as possible with the moderator.

IS A *BABEL FISH* ENOUGH?

The babel fish is the universal translator in book *The Hitchhiker's Guide to the Galaxy.* Are machine translation tools getting close to that science fiction scenario?

A blog post at Big Think suggested this scenario for a visit to Iraq. "You'll walk into a small diner on the street and look at the menu, all of which is written in Arabic. However, when you look at it, the entire menu appears to be in English making it perfectly easy for you to choose a dish. The software in your contact lenses recognizes the Arabic words, and translates them into English for you to view." (Parag and Ayesha Khanna, Big Think)

Figure 7.2

That future may be closer than we think. A number of translation tools are getting close to real-time translation. The WordLens app (http://questvisual.com) does on-the-fly translations of written signs. Google Translate (http://translate.google.com) has a conversation mode that handles both text and speech between two languages (only English and Spanish as of early 2011).

It all sounds great, but there are dissenting voices. A lively discussion on Big Think suggested that there is more to learning a language than just translating the words.

> Communication is partly verbal, but we also have to live "in the moment" of the communicative transaction, taking into account body language, facial expression, gesture, context, cultural signifiers, and nuance. ... Learning a language is the gateway to the culture of the people who speak it.
>
> **John Connor**

> As someone who has developed near native skill in Japanese ... Having learned a language far separated from my own, I have expanded my ability to see the big picture, to imagine new ideas, to think in ways that simply would have been impossible or unlikely with only my native language.
>
> **Chris Harrington**

You can read the full discussion in You Will Never Have to Study a Foreign Language Khanna, Parag and Ayesha (2011) http://bigthink.com/ideas/26386. There is a video demonstrating how Google Translate might be used in real time on YouTube at http://www.youtube.com/watch?v=oyRQnfllv6Y

Interpreters

Interpreters can make or break a session. If you do research across languages, simultaneous interpreters are a fact of life. A good one can seem completely transparent, but the quality is vey mixed. When the quality is bad, it can be deadly. Some things to watch for are:

- The deadly monotone. Interpreters who give you a flow of words with no connection to the way the participant actually spoke. This happens more with interpreters working "behind the glass" than when they are in the room with the participant. When it does, it can be very difficult to stay engaged.
- Too much summarizing. Interpreters who summarize answers or interject their own explanations may not be accurately representing what the participant is saying.
- Dialects and accents. Interpreters who speak a different local dialect may have trouble with the terminology or accent of participants, or even of the moderator.

Poor interpretation can be frustrating, but it doesn't have to completely ruin a session. If you were there to observe the interaction and see the body language and emotion, you will probably be able to (as Henning Fischer described it) "discern what was important to local audiences" by thinking about the entire data set.

Modern Formats and Local Tastes

An article in Forbes about global retailer Carrefour's hypermarkets in China said, "East and West splash against each other. Tanks of live fish, eels, bullfrogs, and turtles dominate the fresh food sections, while vacuum-packed strips of bacon and slices of pepperoni lie in refrigerated cases a short distance away. Modern formats mix with local tastes." (Child 2006)

If you do use an interpreter, make sure both the team and the participant understand the roles: who is running the interview or conversation, who is taking notes. In China, for example, when foreigners are part of the team, people might assume that they are the most important people and try to talk to them. If your plan was to quietly observe the interaction, that won't work. Alternatively, participants may want to talk only to the local people on the team, even if they are just there to take notes.

A good interpreter can also help with cultural interpretation Doug Wang gave us a good example of this. "In a Hong Kong supermarket, live animals are killed on the spot. To the Westerner this might look brutal, with the blood an so on. But to a Chinese person, this is about freshness and good meat."

A final word of warning is not to make assumptions about language and whether you can work with participants in English. Better to have someone ready to translate.

One of the assumptions I made in a project in Hong Kong was that if we screen for people who can speak English then we won't need a translator. We realized after the first interview that "speaking English" means different things for different people and we *will* need a translator in some cases. This wasn't just about being able to speak English, but also the shades of meanings and subtle variations in language. The way you articulate things is different from culture to culture. Having someone there who can really tease out that subtlety is super important. We had expectations that we would be able to know everything people said. I realize now that this was a hubristic and wrong approach. I think also even just having someone local who understands the subtlety of the culture can really help you analyze what was said during that study.

Rachel Hinman

Allow Things to Uncover Themselves

We worked one project about how people create solutions in their everyday life—all kinds of solutions, from coordinating who picks up the kids from daycare to what to get from the supermarket to how to remember ideas that you might come up with sometime during the day or night.

We selected people through snowball contacts, letting each person we talked to suggest others. This technique for finding people works for us because there is a stronger motivation.

We have a little conversation before we actually go visit them. We ask them what kind of situations we could join them in. In this case, it let us select places to meet that gave us diversity in locations that we would visit: some people at work, perhaps join some people while in traffic, going home from work, or going to pick up the kids from school. Then we also ask them to do a little bit of homework, such as making notes about an average week day and an average weekend day.

When we get there, we just have a conversation. We have some topics that we want to address but we do this in the form of a conversation. We really work to create an atmosphere that is their everyday life together with them as opposed to them sitting upright and giving us the right answers to our questions.

It's really important we understand all these layers in people's everyday life and how it connects to the culture they live in. If we are surprised or confused by something they tell us, we ask them about it. We want to make stories that are quite clear, although they might also be complex.

A sign that one of these visits is a success is when people tell us that they learned quite a bit about themselves as well during that afternoon. We understand a remark like that as meaning that they went a bit deeper in their thinking about their everyday life, that they intuitively know but never expressed very clearly, perhaps. It means we have uncovered layers of understanding about their everyday life.

Bas Raijmakers and Geke van Dijk

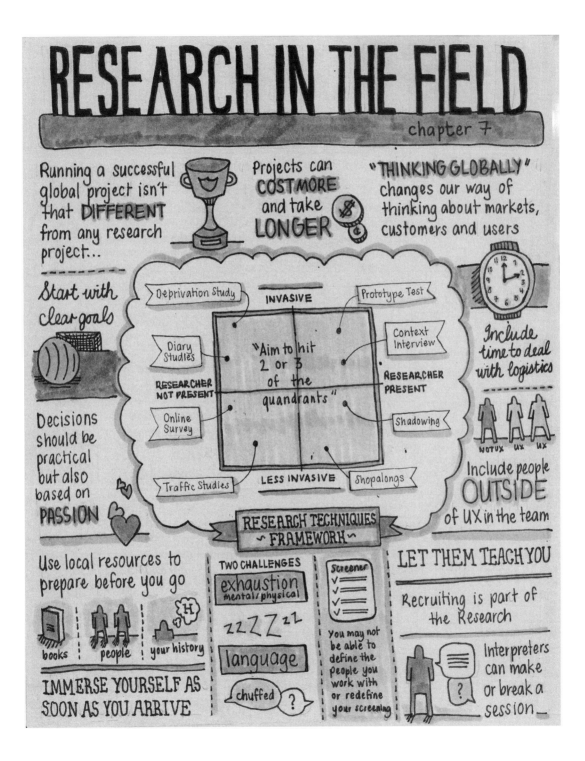

BRINGING IT HOME

The walls are covered with photos and sticky notes. The table holds a pile of objects, from snack food containers to transit tickets collected on a research trip. As the team shares their insights Jai is leading a group of managers, designers, and developers in connecting all this material to their own experiences and brainstorming how it might apply to their work.

Once the research is done, how do you make sense of what you've learned? More importantly, how do you share what you learned with the full team and make it part of the background knowledge for everyone in the company? A simple report of the data won't do. This isn't just user success percentages or task analysis: global research reports have to communicate the nuance of cultural similarities and differences.

These reports have to communicate strongly enough to allow people who were not part of the journey to share the experience. The entire team needs to hear and synthesize the research in a way that can help them with their own work.

That challenge has led to *un-reports* that recreate the immersive environment from the field. Photos, sketches, and other artifacts all share the details of the experience. Personas and stories put a face on the research data.

For some, it has also changed the daily routine of running a UX research project. Instead of waiting until all research is done, daily debriefs get insights out before they are lost to information overload and the normal process of forgetting detail.

This chapter examines some of the techniques for sharing cultural knowledge in a way that is useful and can influence the design process.
- How do we gather our conclusions in an effective way?
- What goes into a global research report?
- Can the reporting environment help the team share the experience?
- How do we synthesize the insights from research for design?

Coming to Conclusions

Global research projects often involve many people. Some are part of the research team, but others are from a wider circle: project and product managers, marketing and sales, or other parts of the project team. As you analyze the work, you need their participation in coming to conclusions.

Analysis with the Whole Team

The research team has been on both a literal journey and a journey of understanding. When you are bringing back insights on other cultures, you may find that you need to make an extra effort to connect what you have learned with people on the project who did not go along on the research. When you include everyone, no matter what role each person played, you have an opportunity to build a shared understanding of the research results, and make it more likely that the results will be incorporated into the design or product.

> The most important moment is when we get back together with the full client team and we try to make sense of those stories. Then we try to cocreate the insights with them, so we're really careful that we don't do the whole analysis ourselves and then present polished off insights. What we do is structure material so that it's possible in like a day workshop with a team, to dive into it and make sense of it. We cluster it, we organize it, we make something like an exhibition out of it. Those workshops are really, really important for people in the client team to understand what these stories tell.
>
> **Bas Raijmakers and Geke van Dijk**

This process can take many forms. One is to create a workshop with the whole team—people who went on the research and everyone else—that acts as a virtual immersion. Anjali Kelkar makes this process active. First, she assembles a collection of photos, and shows them with a 30-second commentary on each one. As they watch, everyone writes down their own observations and insights for a guided exercise to come up with inputs for the product design. The value of this approach is that no one can say, "Where did you get this concept from?" "The answer is that *they* did. Half an hour ago. As a researcher, you may have these ideas—you are always looking for solutions. But this process makes translating research into action a team process that engages the client as a stake holder rather than a detached process that a consultant delivers as a research and design package."

Debriefing as You Go

Debriefing as you go keeps the information fresh. In some projects, researchers try to avoid coming to conclusions until all the data collection is complete. In the tradition of carefully constructed experimentation, they don't want to bias the results by introducing their own reflections. User research—especially the type of field work that makes up much global UX research with the goal of informing design—is different. It draws on the techniques of ethnography where writing up notes is part of a researcher's regular work. In the rich world outside the lab, the video recording can't capture every detail and impression.

Many texts on collecting ethnographic data emphasize the importance of writing notes at the end of each day to start the process of synthesizing your more cryptic scratch notes and assimilating what you have seen. This process of reflection can also help you improve your interviewing and observations in the following days.

For many of the people we talked to, the daily debriefing is not only a way to stay on top of the work, but also a way to help the team sort through the mass of information. Even before the notes are compiled and analyzed, it can be valuable to get together to "sit around the campfire and tell your stories," as Henning Fischer put it. It can help them put the research into context and see that others share their perspectives on what they have learned.

This daily work of collecting your notes can be an informal debriefing or a short set of written notes. It's important to build in time for a debrief after each interview, even if it's just an informal way to capture information while it's fresh. Some people follow a practice of writing daily summaries to quickly collect both details and impressions about what they've seen. It's important to do that as you go along, so that there is not this mountain of writing and recollection to do once you finish. Skip this step, and you risk losing precious insights.

Analysis Over Distance

Distance can make the analysis work more difficult. When the team members come from many different places, they don't have the luxury of taking all the notes, recordings, photos, and other material they have collected back to one place to go through it. When the team is global, each person may head home to a different place where distance makes the tight collaboration of analysis more difficult.

> Another challenge is to make sure that we come up with our conclusions very shortly after data collection. So we are not going back to our home offices before we finish summarizing the study. Everyone stays there for a couple of days to make sure that all of our insights and understandings are in place before we come back. Otherwise, it's a challenge of time zones again, and coming back to our "day jobs." We don't want to lose what we have there.
>
> **Tomer Sharon**

If your company is still already used to the diversity of cultures, then sharing research insights can be relatively straightforward. But, as Anne Kaikkonen has found, "When there are people who have lived in one environment and have more difficulties in understanding the diversity, then it is definitely more challenging. And the best way in making people understand something that they haven't experienced themselves, is to create a story."

When the research team disperses, with everyone going back to their own office, they can tell the story through their own, first-hand, experience. The benefits are not just better results, but a deeper understanding of the value of doing user research at all.

Creating a Richer Picture

What kind of report is the most effective? A formal report may be a requirement in more formal organizations or as a way of completing a consulting project. But a written report is not the only way to bring back what you have learned to make sure it is really heard.

In our interviews, people talked about many different ways to do this. Although the details varied, the common theme was finding ways to get people involved in activities so they can engage with the material.

For some, a workshop is one way to change the dynamic from passively listening to actively creating a new culture. For Daniel, this was a shift in how he thinks about his role. It was a success when a client said "When you said *workshop*, you really meant *workshop*." He explains it this way. "What they meant was that they weren't sitting in a room listening to a presenter 'blah blah blah' all day. This was a workshop where we're going to do things together. We're going to tell stories together and design together. My role is to facilitate it in a way that I'm creating a shift of culture, right in that room."

This approach lets you communicate a research report from the bottom up. When everyone is allowed to talk, you can start with the stories and insights from the research experience, but anyone can ask questions or dive into the specifics more deeply. You may be framing the discussion around themes in the data, but having an open conversion lets you connect the details of the research data to why it's important or how it impacts design.

Immersive Reporting

So what does a report look like if it's not a pile of paper and presentation slides? The answer is that reporting can be an immersive experience.

The first step is creating an environment. It can be as simple as materials pinned to big sheets of cardboard. The important thing for Marc Rettig is that "the meeting happens in a place surrounded by all the content you are going to present, but in a very visual way. When you're guided through it, there's a lot more in there than you thought when you first looked at it. The posters stay up, so for a week afterwards, people gather around them and have conversations they wouldn't otherwise have had."

At a formal company like a bank, this sort of rich, creative space can change how people think. When Kimberly Wiessner brings people to the UX team's creative space, "They walk in and first of all, every window, every wall is covered with paper and scribbles and feedback and sticky notes. People casually having meetings and discussions about projects, getting feedback from each other while they work. When you take people out of our formal culture and bring them here, it opens up like a door to a world that most people in the bank can't even imagine. But the most interesting thing is that we have a lot of heads of business groups who want to be more involved. They want to be a part of this process because it's really fun. It gives them energy."

At Google, Tomer Sharon creates what he calls a *research expo*. An expo is a full-day event during which people experience the

---

Engaging Teams with Rich Reporting
You can read more about research expos in Engaging Teams with Rich Reporting: Recipe for a research findings expo. In UPA's User Experience magazine http://www.usabilityprofessionals.org

research instead of reading about it. They take over a room for a day and set up a self-guided exhibit of posters, artifacts, and videos from the research. People can wander through it like a gallery, taking in all in. Members of the study team are there to talk about the findings with them.

Connect to the Research

One of the wonderful things about making the report immersive and interactive is that you are creating an experience that allows everyone to be part of the report. The goal is to help everyone connect to what you have learned. This also allows everyone to be part of the story, no matter what their role in the project.

For any research, the goal of the reporting process is to bring back what you have learned in a form that people can connect to. When it's presented as *just data* it's harder to make that connection. If there was a single common thread among all the interviews, it was that it's important to humanize the data, and put it into a context.

After a project of more than 50 interviews around financial needs, Steve Baty presented the results as a set of customer journeys with anecdotes and photos to tell a story. "It can be hard for people in the business, or even the designers, to care about someone's experience if you haven't made a connection with them. The key was that we talked about individuals, and went out of our way to bring the people we met into the presentation."

Project Rooms Let You Share Stories

Ziba once worked on a brand design project for a global sportswear company in China. Bill didn't get to go to China, but as we talked to him about this project, we were struck at how much he had absorbed, even secondhand. It speaks to how Ziba infused the research into the rest of the company.

"Every single project has a room dedicated to them. The project team can just go in there and work. It's all magnetic whiteboards so you can put stuff up, draw on the walls—just make a massive, beautiful mess to try and figure out what is the core essence in this project. Typically, there's a ton of imagery pinned up on the wall. These could be photos that were taken in the field. We took thousands and thousands of photos in China. You cull through the ones that inspire them somehow, print them out, put them on the wall.

We buy a lot of products as well—shampoo bottles and toothbrushes and random books—bring those into the room. Actual, tangible things that can remind you of what it's like to walk through a store or be in a person's house. You're trying to recreate as much of the environment as possible, given the massive limitations that you're in a conference room in the United States as opposed to being on the street in China.

We don't just put stuff up and leave it there. There's a constant evolution. Things go up on a wall, then you have of session where you try to move things around. You're sorting it out: here's all these images that have a theme of, let's say play, or social events, or whatever.

There's a lot of cross-project sharing. In the Ziba lobby, there is an installation with a thousand photos spread across six different themes to summarize the overall findings. We also encourage people to visit other project rooms and just get a sense of what's going on. Once a month, there's a happy hour tour when people present what's going on in their projects."

Bill DeRouchey

Telling the Story

There's something about stories. They are a tangible, simple way of presenting the results of any research that can have great impact on the organization. Whether you use words, photographs, sketches, or video, it all comes down to telling a rich story. The more material you have, the easier the story is to create and the more it communicates a depth of understanding. More importantly, stories are especially effective when you are describing a "foreign" place.

> When I look back at my practice, stories have always been the most effective way to communicate. Think about returning home from a research trip. What do you want to do? You don't want to hide yourself away for a couple of days writing reports. No. Instead, you want to hang out with people and talk to them and tell them stories of what happened. People love hearing stories.
>
> **Robert Barlow-Busch**

Stories through Photographs

Photographs are one way to trigger stories about the research. On any trip, you learn so much more than *just the facts*. One of the hardest things to communicate is the *feeling* of a different place, the many details you observe that add up to a sense of what that place is like. Photographs—lots of photographs—can help you do this. Most researchers bring back a lot of visual materials so that they have specific images to help inspire the design and tell the story through photographs.

Perhaps you come back, as Marc Rettig did, thinking that there was a very different sense of personal space and safety. That the boundaries are different. You can use an image to support that. "Here's a family of five stacked up on a motorcycle with no helmets or anything, just riding in this dense traffic."

Of course, it's more than just pointing a camera. With digital cameras, anyone can take a good enough photo. The trick is finding the right image and the right words to carry the audience to a place and help them see the meaning behind the pictures. It's also a chance to focus on the environment around the thing you are researching.

> I read an article about how wonderful it was that anyone with a camera can go out and get cultural insights and just stand on a street corner. In an hour, they took something like 84 pictures of people riding bicycles. But it didn't occur to them to take a picture of the people who were walking. It's easy to focus on the people

Stories Are More Than Narrative
Stories describe events, but also explain actions, and set them into a context that helps you understand why they happened. A good story weaves together causes and effects in a narrative so we can best remember them. It captures context and tacit knowledge and does so more efficiently than any other form of communication. Whitney Quesenbery and Kevin Brooks (2010)

doing the thing you are researching, but in that local context, we need to ask why people aren't doing the thing. That can highlight the differences in perspective. Choosing not to do something is just as big a choice as choosing to do something.

Steve Baty

Stories with Video

A well-edited video can tell a powerful story.

Film is really necessary for the work that we do, so that we can communicate to a lot of other people—inside the company, the clients, the design teams that we work with. We really need to have a strong visual story. The films come out the best when we make those stories together with participants as opposed to just about them. That's why we take this approach of first having the conversation to explore topics with them, and then making decisions together. We organize this filming with them—script it if you like. We work out how the story could best be told as opposed to just following them around and then later try to edit something out of that.

Bas Raijmakers and Geke van Dijk

However, only a few people we interviewed used video as an integral part of their process. Most mentioned it, but rarely had the time in their projects to do much with it. "We always collect it," Henning Fischer told us, "but the amount of time that it takes us to go back into audio or video makes it too difficult. We always have it for backup, and sometimes pull out a short clip, for example if someone says something really brilliant that you want to show the client." It also might be just that as a time-based medium, video is not as immediate and accessible for everyone on the team as a wall full of images. These walls become triggers for a kind of immersion in the users' environment for the whole team.

Stories through Sketches

Designers often carry a sketch book with them everywhere and are constantly sketching. Even if you think you can't draw, the idea is a good one.

My personal way of sharing information is through stories I can tell about research that I've seen. I keep a sketch book with me 24/7, and write down things that I see customers do. Sketch things, write down quotes, things like that. Any time, I'll open my notebook to the page of the research and let people read it … let people try to reach through and understand it.

Kimberly Wiessner

Sketches can be simple, a way of capturing common scenes from the slice of life you studied. They can be different than photographs, because the act of creating the drawing lets you focus on a particular item, or emphasize something in the scene, guiding people's intention to what is important for the story you are trying to tell.

Acting Out the Story

We've talked about using an immersive environment or visual images to tell a story. But stories can be part of a traditional presentation, too. For one recent project, Tomer Sharon wrote two stories based on quotes from participants. "They are pretty long, about 15 minutes each. In a presentation, I tell these stories and then recap the main messages. I'm trying to make people experience what I found, but also think about the two or three main messages." It makes the whole presentation more memorable.

The request was a slightly unusual one: a new client asked us to bust myths about their user segments, and move the internal clients—designers, marketers, engineers, and product managers—beyond rehashing clichéd beliefs about these customers. In response, we convened a workshop modeled after a daytime television talk show.

We worked with a research team to assemble a rich narrative, including back story, attitudes toward technology, purchasing behavior, and so on. Bullet points like "active in social media" became plot points like "I Facebooked my best friend when I got home from work."

The researchers took to the stage at this workshops (billed, with no zombie-irony as *Segments Come Alive*) and introduced themselves in the guise of their characters, and we played the role of ethnographers-as-broadcast interlocutors to draw out more personal details from these characters. Then we turned things over to the audience, who had their own questions about the segments.

The experience was an exercise in stepping outside of our comfort zones (even as the actors confronted newly highlighted gaps in their insights about and even their empathy for customers) but it was refreshing and invigorating for everyone, as these segments went from corporate documentation to lively stories about people.

Steve Portigal

> You can also get people from the team to act out the stories, using a technique called informance, described in Brenda Laurel's book *Design Research: Methods and Perspective* (2003).

PERSONAS FOR CULTURAL USES

We created one persona per role, but we made sure to create at least one persona from Singapore and one from India, to remind the product development teams that our products span across different countries and cultures. In addition we integrated any cultural differences into the personas without including a separate section that called out cultural differences. We did this by incorporating findings from each country in a realistic scenario for the given country of the persona under creation. For example, Short Message Service (SMS) was used frequently as a work task in Singapore and India, but not nearly as much in the United States. However, we still incorporated SMS into the US personas because we knew this was something important to include in the future mobile applications. This approach allowed for a single voice for each persona.

(Snyder, Sampanes, White, Hnilo 2010)

Stories through Personas

More and more projects use personas as a way to present a deeper understanding of people—what their background is, what environments they live or work in, social connections … whatever is important for the project. Personas are also a good way to communicate the context, whether it's a specific culture or details of a workplace. The details and texture can be revealed through the persona.

In a project comparing call centers in New Zealand and the United States, Peter Grierson wanted to show the product team the lives of the people they affected on a daily basis. He set up workstations to show what was on the screen, and told the stories through the proxies of personas. One of the side benefits of using personas was that blending observations from several people helped protect the privacy of the individuals and companies.

Personas can help you think through differences in social context. "Imagine you are in India." Jhilmil Jain created stories about how a remote control is shared. "Not just anyone can change the channel. Your father is sitting there, and he controls it. You can't just make the decision on your own." She used these stories to create scenarios for different contexts, and then, given that context, think about how to design.

Stories can also be a way to show how one individual might have several different ways of interacting with other people. As an Canadian Muslim who grey up in a multicultural part of Toronto, Kaleem Khan says that, "there might be one way of interacting within the family, another for friends from the neighborhood, a third at work, and still others for socializing with people from work. These are not rules, but natural variations in human behavior based on context. You have to understand that a person is more than just someone who's trying to perform a task, as we too often assume. Humans are not unidimensional, but have many roles, responsibilities, and perspectives that affect how they use a product. Our designs need to account for their varied contexts and frames of reference."

The point, as Bas Raijmakers and Geke van Dijk emphasize, is that you have to be clear what question you are trying to answer, and what point you are trying to make. "The difference between personas and marketing segmentation is that the personas are meant to inspire thinking about new services. In a world with a more active role for the consumer, companies need a way to have a different relationship with their customers. This is part of the creative process."

TELLING STORIES REVEALS CONTEXT

Consider an iceberg. When we tell or hear a story, all that is understood about that story is the tip of the iceberg seen above the waterline, unless we also know all the context that is hidden below! When we know the context, the story often takes on different or fuller meanings or understandings.

When storytelling across cultures, we need to take into consideration several things: meaning, context, cultural gaps, important or difficult words/phrases and expressions, worldview, the plot/theme and intended meaning of the story, idiomatic expressions, historical implications, implicit information, frame of reference and shared frame of reference, and so on. In short, we need to do a lot of homework! (All of this kind of takes the fun out of just telling a story, doesn't it?) Anyway, cultural anthropologists repeatedly say that a culture's stories reveal worldview. And I strongly believe this. I also believe that it is stories that shape worldview. Therefore, if you aren't an "insider" of that culture, sometimes it is hard to understand and tell its stories.

In cross-cultural situations, it is important that the storyteller conveys to the audience that he or she understands the audience and its culture, at least somewhat. Then, the stories in some way need to touch on that audience and its culture—telling within that shared context or shared frame of knowledge, experience, and meaning. The audience appreciates it when it can relate to your stories, when they don't seem so foreign that the audience can't relate to them. If "foreign" stories are told to illustrate, inform, or enlighten, they really must be told in ways that they can be understood and appreciated!

Be magical, be mystical, be enchanting, be entertaining, be informative. And be YOU. You are the greatest translator from one culture (yours) to another.

Steve Evans is a cultural researcher who specializes in cross-cultural and oral communications. Photography is an integral part of his work. This is an excerpt from "Meaning is Found in Context" (2008). You can follow Steve's photography at http://babasteve. blogspot.com/.

Carrying the Conversation Forward

The ultimate goal is to make a connection between the research and how it can be used to move a project forward. That conversation starts with the informal debriefings and is continued through the work of analyzing and sharing the results. During that process, what Bas and Geke call the moment of synthesis occurs, when something triggers an understanding and becomes a new idea. "When these ideas come up, we often do an exercise when we say, 'Let's step again into the shoes of the participants and let's invite them to give a response on these ideas.' It is always possible to think, 'Let's look at this idea from the perspective of Toby. What would Toby think of this?' The idea is to move from the observations, the field work, the insights, and use them to generate new service concepts."

At this moment, all the rich materials you have gathered really pay off. Instead of sitting around a table with a pile of paper in their hands, this moment takes place surrounded by all the photos and stories that you have structured for the event.

One other piece of advice comes from Rachel Hinman: Limit the number of key points. "I find that people can't handle more than five major implications. After a study, you can come up with five directives or design principles that explain what we have heard, what it means, and why it matters to our project. From there, you can gain insight into how you can expand on those principles into some sort of expression in design."

Design Synthesis
"Design is that act of problem solving—of appropriating formal qualities into a new design idea that fulfills the stated criteria and adds value to the human condition. Synthesis is a sensemaking process that helps the designer move from data to information, and from information to knowledge." Jon Kolko (2010)

A Broader Conversation

The last step is to find ways to carry the conversation out into the company. The research may have been aimed at one project or one problem, but some of the cultural knowledge can be used in many projects. One of the reasons to bring other stakeholders on research trips is so that they can be the ones to share stories about what they saw. It may have more impact coming from a direct colleague.

You can also make a conscious point of bringing information from research into any conversation. When Kimberly Wiessner is in any meeting, "I can recall things I've seen in research and speak to those things. I think bringing those tidbits of information back into the business daily grind of whatever it is we're trying to accomplish is really, really important."

All of this aims to create a larger discussion about whether we are creating the best experience for the customer, and whether we have a rich enough global understanding of the customer to ensure that we're delivering on the best experience.

DESIGN FOR A GLOBAL AUDIENCE

IN THIS CHAPTER

When you start to design, it's the moment of truth. Have you done enough research to be read for all the decisions about the design? Are you confident in understanding both what is different and what is the same about all of the users? Do you understand the words they use to think about the things they will do with the product you are creating?

At the end of the day, a global strategy must produce products that will work in all the local markets where they are sold and used. This means that any design is "multipoint." Kevin Cheng summed it up this way: "You design for the market. Thinking globally is really about thinking locally. It's not about sitting somewhere and thinking about all these cultures and markets. It's about actually being in those areas, and serving those markets. Having people who live that culture, involved in the product."

Hopefully by this point, you've got a rich set of actionable design insights. Once you have done your homework global design isn't so different from any other UX design, but with a few extras to consider:

- Plan for globalization
- Decide on your global strategy
- Get the language right
- Create a good local experience

Plan for Globalization

Global work adds to the criteria for success. It's not just "can people complete the tasks or use the product effectively." Now you want to know whether it fits comfortably into all of their local contexts, whether it gives them a sense of trust, or matches the way they think about the product, across languages and cultures.

Technically, our lives would be a lot easier if globalization meant that things were the same everywhere, but probably don't want that, right? Robert Barlow-Busch said, "Personally, I want to celebrate our differences. I love that there are differences and want there to continue to be differences. That's what makes life interesting for all of us."

> The thing with global is that you end up with this crazy mix of similarities that you can work with. And differences that become opportunities to create variations and differentiation in your work. But there are also things that can bite you in the ass if you assume that something will be different or assume that something will be the same, and don't actually go look at it.
>
> **Steve Baty**

As Will Evans said, "Even a simple product becomes complex when it is used in a global context." You have to get the basics right so you can accommodate the added complexity of multi-point global UX design.

Research Homework

The first basic is to do the work to know about and understand anything unique in the market, whether it's a complex mix of variations on a legal or financial system or something as simple to identify as the direction of the writing.

This work should start with what people called "basic hygiene," or the things that are easy to discover, or the things at the bottom level of a hierarchy of needs—in other words the basic facts about each location or culture where the product will be sold and used. You probably don't need to run design research sessions to learn this sort of largely factual information.

You probably also want to do a review of any current products, to find out how well they are already adapted for a global audience. What you learn might surprise you.

> It's not even cultural, it's a very practical difference. In the US, when you talk about billing, you always bill in one currency and it's very straightforward. But in Europe, they have multiple currencies, and when you try to bill clients, it becomes a problem.

If we don't offer solutions in our product, they will simply not use our product. They will go to another product that does it better. And we're just talking about billing, not even the reason they bought our product. They just couldn't do it with our product, because we only deal with one currency.

Tomer Sharon

Build In Globalization from the Start

Global products almost always require local variations, even if this is just translating the text, converting currency, and having appropriate formats for time and other measurements. This requires the underlying technical structures for internationalization. Without them, you can only adapt to each new market with custom coding and each variation is an entirely different program.

If you are just starting out with a new product, the best advice we heard was to plan for globalization from the beginning, no matter how slowly you think you will actually need to create local variations. Unfortunately, in the rush to market, many programs are written for one location and one language, making them harder to globalize later.

At Constant Contact, the product was not designed at all to be an international product. The entire interface is in English, so the international customers we have are mostly in English-speaking countries. The challenge isn't so much cultural as getting the functionality right. We're starting to redesign the forms to prepare for internationalization, doing things like moving the field labels to a position where they will work in all languages.

Sarah Bloomer

DEFINITIONS

Everyone seems to have their own definitions for localization, internationalization, and globalization. For some, *localization* is just translation; for others it's the entire process. These definitions are adapted from the W3C Internationalization Activity (www.w3.org/international).

- **Internationalization** is the design of the product and the technical structures that enable localization. It happens in the code, for example, by using variables to control how temperature or distances are stored and displayed or to insert text from a separate file for each language.
- **Localization** is the process of adapting a product for different countries or locales. It is sometimes limited to translation of any text—changing the words from one language to another, taking

into consideration dialects or other variations in a language, phrasing and even communication styles. It also includes rules for formatting dates, numbers, and currency; and the use of symbols, icons or other design elements.

- **Globalization** is the process of customizing or adapting a general product design and work flow to an audience based on local or cultural differences. It may also include alternative modules for functions to meet local needs or other changes based on ways of doing business. In many Muslim countries, for example, you can use your mobile phone to find Mecca.

Cultural Audits

If you are starting on a globalization project for an existing product, you might want to start with a cultural audit of the user experience to see how much it might need localization.

> I've talked about the importance of cultural differences in software design for 10 years, and I'm seeing signs of the ice breaking. This year, we got a project to do a cultural audit of a software product before it was translated into another language. Our audit included all of the graphics, icons, metaphor and terminology to identify idioms that might not translate well because they are sensitive, dangerous, illegal, or offensive. These sorts of projects are an indication that some people in some companies are beginning to wake up to the need to look at cultural issues. I think it's more than an isolated event.
>
> **Aaron Marcus**

In your audit, remember to look for commonalities, not just differences. Adrian Hallam, who regularly deals with projects in over 20 countries, finds that he spends more time focusing on what his audiences have in common, regardless of culture. "With big projects, there are so many details that you can get drowned if you are not focused on a clear vision. When the team knows the goal, and believes in the purpose of the project, they are more likely to be successful."

> People looking at the skills needed for global projects tend to focus on understanding and adapting to cultural differences. While I agree this is essential to at least some extent, I personally feel this can be difficult for projects dealing with 20+ countries every week. It can be tiring at best and damaging at worst to try and adapt, or compromise, to that each culture. Perhaps a better focus is to spend more time looking at what people have in common and to focus on leveraging these commonalities. It sounds quite easy,

however with big projects there are so many details to get drowned in that it helps to stay deliberately focused on this goal. The most obvious and best commonality is the power of a common vision.

When the teams know what and why they are trying to do something - and believe in its purpose and results - then success is likely to be the result. Integrity, consistency and reliability are also obvious candidates for values common to all people. Also, for a good leader, although general soft skills and skills to influence people are critically important, they don't take the place of keeping on top of industry latest news and developments on a daily basis. People are generally happy to be led or influenced by someone who they see as knowledgeable and relevant.

Adrian Hallam

Content Strategy

When you are planning an international web site, both the design and content have to be manageable, maintainable, and scalable. That takes planning, and thinking about the capabilities of the organization, the type of information, and the resources needed for ongoing maintenance of the site.

When I worked on a project internationalizing the web site for International Paper, I started with the information, determining what information needed to be shared across sites, and what information needed to be local. Then, I wanted to know who was going to manage the content. If you are sending content out to local offices to translate, how will it be kept up to date? If you are relying on those offices to create content, will they have the staff to manage it? Cultural issues are important, but you also have to be practical and make sure you find the balance between the ideal and something that is achievable.

Sarah Bloomer

Decide on Your Strategy

Before you can decide on a UX strategy, you have to have a product strategy. Maren Pyenson said it very clearly. "It's difficult to build a successful international product if you don't have a clear business goal. If you don't have clear goals and a way to measure them, you don't know if your strategy has been effective or not."

Companies may start with the one market, usually the country or region where they are based. Some products are initially tailored for the North American market because it's such a large source of revenue, not only from US companies, but also from some based in Asia. Even companies that intend to create global products may tailor a product for one market first, or make it a priority. Pabini Gabriel-Petit has seen this in projects with smaller companies.

> It's just too expensive to start with a fully global approach, so companies often design for the US and hope it will work well for others, then expand their commitment to designing explicitly for other markets as they can afford to. For example, when I was VP of User Experience at scanR, we created a global version of the product that was mainly targeted toward users in the US. But we also created a version of the product especially for the Japanese market, where high-quality cameras were more common in mobile phones early on. That was a key market for us, so worth the investment.
>
> **Pabini Gabriel-Petit**

Or, companies may have a global strategy that includes many different countries or regions. A UX strategy in this case might avoid too much focus on a single region, or might focus more consciously on research in markets with more cultural variations. By gathering design insights from a variety of locations, these companies start with a stronger base of product concepts that will work around the world. The research phase may become longer and more complex, however.

Managing a Global Brand

From all the stories we heard, three basic approaches to managing a global brand emerged:
- **One product**: The product is designed for a home market and sold globally with only minor localization.
- **Local control**: Although all part of a global brand, each product is really a franchise in its own market, and makes its own design decisions.
- **Global templates with local variations**: A global UX group creates and manages a set of templates that both set a global standard and allow for local adaptations.

Each of these approaches is reflected in other aspects of the corporate and design management, from web governance to how UX standards are set.

Lisa Welchman, of Welchman-Pierpoint, who specializes in strategies for web governance suggests that there are three basic

Web governance models

Lisa Welchman's slides showing the organizational structures for different web governance models are on Slideshare. (www.slideshare.net/welchmanpierpoint/three-web-governance-models-that-work)

models for managing and setting policies for a large corporate web site:
- **Empire**: All control of the web site, including design and content, is centralized in one group.
- **Confederation**: Loose relationship between business units with little central control, and voluntary participation in web standards.
- **Federation**: Business units work together to agree on how the web will be governed. The central group is given authority to manage shared resources.

When we match the approach and the brand or web governance model, the management of the global UX design falls into line as well. There are, of course, both benefits and drawbacks to each.

Approach	UX Design	Governance Model
One product	Centrally managed design	Empire
Local control	Local designs based on loose standards	Confederation
Global templates	Centrally managed templates for local designs	Federation

One Product, with Minor Localization

These products are typically designed for a primary market, and then sold in other places with only minor variations. This approach assumes that there is little variation in how the product is used or understood. It can be effective for products or services:
- That serve niche markets with little local variation in task or process
- That are used primarily by people from similar cultures
- Like luxury brands, where aspiration to the values of the home culture is part of the appeal
- That are largely hardware-based products, designed to minimize manufacturing costs

Online UX tools are an example of this approach. Tools from the United Kingdom, Spain, Australia, New Zealand, the United States, and more all serve this market with little visible trace of their origin. Hardware such as consumer appliances and computer hardware are difficult and expensive to localize deeply, except by creating completely different products.

Figure 9.1 Twitter is a global product. It is translated into several languages, but the site design is the same. Besides the language, the only localized element of the home page is the pictures of the people with recent tweets at the bottom of the home page (Twitter.com in English, Japanese, Russian, Turkish).

Taking a "one-product" approach might mean that the company does not have the resources, or is not mature enough, to consider the global market for its products. This does not mean the product will be a failure, of course. The product might be able to build from early success to become a global product.

Another reason to maintain a strong central design is that part of the appeal of the product might be the association with the culture of the primary market.

Some brands have a very centralized communication. Louis Vuitton, for example, runs advertising all around the world that is produced, and carefully controlled, from the center. Luxury products tend to be the same in all markets because people are mainly buying into the aspirational value of the brand. For more general daily products, such as shampoo, their communication is more localized. The advertising blends the emotional and functional benefits of what the brand can do with a local twist to local habits or even ingredients. It really is about understanding both the similarities and the relevant differences.

Mark Webster

For this approach, part of the job of the UX team is to ensure that the UX design works everywhere. User research can help the design be culturally neutral enough to succeed without being specifically adapted to local cultures. One of the roles of the UX manager or international product manager might be to bridge the gap between the central group and local offices.

The danger of this approach is a product that is too inflexible to succeed in many different cultures. It may never be seen as a truly local product, and have difficulty competing for local loyalty. If the central design team does not have a good global research program, it may miss trends or changes in local markets.

Locally Controlled Products

These products are linked by a common brand, but are really local franchises. Yahoo!, for example, is actually a group of independent companies. This approach can be effective for products and services that:

- Have a strong local character, or are based on finding local resources
- Are based on individual preferences that are easily influenced by context or culture
- Are regulated in each country, such as medical or financial services

This approach gives local companies the most control over the layout and content of the site, and allows them to respond quickly to changes in local needs, such as a new competitor.

In some markets, products swing back and forth between copying features or styles from the local market leader and using the global brand to differentiate themselves in the market. Its downside is the difficulty in maintaining a consistent brand or set of features across many different local companies. Even with the best intentions, it can be hard to keep up with developments in so many places and ensure that local products support the global brand.

Figure 9.2 HSBC sites are locally controlled. They share a basic color scheme, but have different—often radically different—layouts and content on the home page. These three home pages are from HSBC Bank Brasil S.A., HSBC Hong Kong, and HBSC-Trinkaus in Germany.

A Global Template with Local Variations

This approach tries to find a middle ground between a single design for all markets and the ability to create variations to meet local needs. This approach works for:

- Digital and physical products that are tied to a local environment, but also require global branding, such as banks, hotels and other travel services
- Products and services that have a similar workflow, but also have strong local variations that need to be addressed

The challenge of this approach is twofold. First, the global template needs to be strong enough to work in all the local markets. This means that the central design group must have a good understanding of all the markets. Second, the template must be flexible enough to allow for variation while maintaining an identifiable brand.

> Marriott has design frameworks in place. It's a comprehensive set of page templates for the global sites. From a cost-benefit basis, it makes sense to have a common code-base. So whenever they can, they use the same code. But, at the same time, they want the local perspective so that when people see the web site they see that we understand their needs, so they make adjustments. As an example, on the US and European sites, they deemphasize the phone channel. This has been successful because customers are used to using e-mail and the Web, and it cuts the use of this expensive channel. But in China and Brazil phone is still very important for making reservations, so they put the phone number more prominently on those sites. Even the largest online travel agency in China, C-TRIP, only gets about 40% of their business from online transactions.
>
> **Wei Ding**

As companies and their products evolve in response to competition and other market forces, the approach to globalization often changes as well. Maren Pyenson says that she sees a back-and-forth between the central HQ and local companies. "It's like two lines running in parallel, but over time they drive apart. Then they come back together again. Differentiation and similarity alternate in a competitive environment." This might be based on research in the local markets, but many other forces are also at work. For example, different content management systems may make it difficult for a local site to adopt the global templates.

Or the local franchise might want to copy the features or interaction style of a successful competitor. This can create inconsistency in the global brand, even as it allows the local site to serve the local market. Jim Neiters, who works for Yahoo!, says

Figure 9.3 Yahoo! is a good example of a global template with local customization. Although many sites use the same template as Yahoo! US, there are also many local variations. Yahoo! US and Yahoo! Korea (a and b), Yahoo!7 in Australia, and Yahoo! Sverige (c and d).

that his response is usually, "Don't change unless you have data that the global template doesn't work." He stresses that every time this issue comes up, you have to make the hard decision between whether the global template or being competitive in the local market is more important.

7 HABITS OF SUCCESSFUL GLOBAL WEB SITES

John Yunker, of ByteLevel Research, is an expert in globalization. He offers this list of good habits for a global company site.

1. **Treat the world equally** - Companies that tend to do the best job at Web globalization are those that view each native market as just one of many markets they serve. This way of thinking permeates the design, functionality, and content of the Web sites, ensuring that a Web user in France has the same experience as a Web user in Florida.

2. **Use a global template** - Your company's Web site may only support four locales today, but three years from now you may have 25 sites to manage. In order to efficiently manage all of these sites, you need a global template.

3. **Direct users to local web sites immediately** - It's not enough to create a localized Web site; you also need to promote it.

4. **Use a permanent global gateway** - Since you cannot guarantee that users will always enter your site through the ".com" front door, you need to be sure they can navigate to their country or language site from anywhere in your Web site.

5. **Use bandwidth wisely** - To be successful globally, Web sites must be ruthlessly economical with graphics, scripting, and other bandwidth-hogging devices.

6. **Act locally** - The best global Web sites create unique local user experiences. From using local models to being sensitive to specific holidays and cultural icons, localization is a significant challenge.

7. **Never stop improving** - Finally, one of the most important traits of the best global Web sites is that they never stand still; they are always being improved.

John Yunker, ByteLevel Research - http://www.bytelevel.com/global/pdfs/7habits.pdf

Getting the Language Right

When we asked about localizing products to different countries or regions, the first concern was often translation. It's the most visible and obvious difference. Some products are localized into as many as 30 or 40 languages, sometimes within a month of a product launch, or even on the same day as the first language (often English).

Language can affect the user interface, with reading direction (reading from right to left instead of left to right or languages that use vertical characters) changing the layout and center of attention. In addition, some languages are more spatially efficient than others, so a design might have to accommodate language expansion. German text, for example, can be 30 percent longer than the equivalent text in English. Planning for the variations in language affect both design and content strategy.

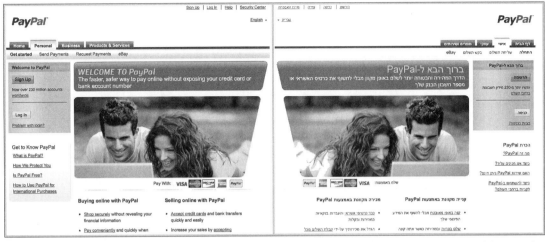

Figure 9.4 PayPal's site for Israel has both English and Hebrew versions. They have the same content and features, but the layouts are mirror images to accommodate the reading direction of the two languages. Even the photo in the center of the screen has been reversed, so that the focus and impact of the faces works in both layout.

Language: A First Step in Localization

Getting the basic language right, with the correct spelling and vocabulary, and correct currency, date, and time formats is just a first step in localization. "You can't worry about the subtlety and persuasion of the text unless you have the text translated into the correct language in the first place," Chris Rourke reminded us. Errors in language can be subtle, such as a slight change in emphasis or an unusual word choice, but they can also create a complete change in the meaning, in the way date format errors do: 7/1/2011 might mean January 7th or July 1st, and the real meaning often cannot be inferred from the context.

There are also political nuances to how language is used in an interface. When she worked on a multinational project to test predictive text entry on mobile phones, Silvia La Hong says they found that on the Arabic language prototypes, typing the letter "I" caused the system to suggest the word "Israel," not the best choice in the current political environment of the Middle East.

Choosing the languages for localization can be a legal requirement in countries more than one official language, such as Switzerland, New Zealand, or Canada. It can also make a statement about your commitment to a language or cultural group. For example, the US version of PayPal, for example, has English, Spanish, French, and Chinese versions. It can be a powerful statement for countries or cultural groups that are small and do not often get localized versions.

There are also variations within a language: French is spoken differently in Canada, France, and Haiti, for example. In the United States, there are many variations of Spanish, so sites either have to appeal to one of the Latino language groups or have to find a neutral language that is not biased toward one group over the other. For the National Cancer Institute, for example, this is not just a matter of voice and tone—there are different words for key medical terms that are important on that site.

Legal Requirements

The words used and how information is presented can even be a legal issue, just as accessibility is. Many countries have laws requiring consumer information such as terms of an agreement to be written in plain language.

- The Consumer Protection Act in South Africa covers brochures to web sites to contracts to ensure that people can make informed choices, and makes businesses responsible for the accuracy of their information.
- Sweden has one of the most comprehensive requirements for plain language in government information and regulations.
- The European Commission has a special interest in clear writing because of how important it is for translation.
- In the United States, the Plain Writing Act requires government to use plain language. Some states require consumer contracts and financial documents such as credit card statements or home mortgage loans to be written in plain English.

Beyond "Just Translating the Words"

Good translations are harder than just changing the words from one language to another. The product also needs to communicate in a way that is appropriate not only for the industry or content topic, but for cultural differences in style and tone.

You may also have to think about how much detail or the types of information to include. Users may expect different amounts of information or information written in different ways. Some cultures accept more informality, even in business relationships, than others.

> When I was in Japan, I remember trying to open a bank account and there were stacks and stacks of things I had to sign. Everything is presented to you—the fine print is not in 8-point type. The bank expected me to go over it and people expect to be shown everything before they commit to something. An amount of information we might see as a bit of an inconvenience was more of an expectation in Japan. I think it had something to do with a trust thing and wanting to be aware of everything they were signing.
>
> **Chris Marmo**

A Good Local Experience

Ultimately, every product has to work for the people we expect to buy it, whether this means a lot of consistency across different markets, or radical differences in the user interface.

> Small and delicate touches of localisation can have a surprisingly large impact on the experience and sales conversion on the site. Local markets develop their own design 'norms' and consumers often display doubts or fears about providers that don't appear to conform to these design standards. In our research, we often see a subtle form of patriotism exists when shoppers draw up short-lists of brands they are considering. Design touches that highlight local customs, pastimes, history and people can lead to higher brand consideration than otherwise might be given to a non-domestic provider. In a good example of this, we have seen French consumers give ING (a Dutch bank) higher consideration because their French home page at the time featured images of a French sports team.
>
> **Peter Ballard**

Global Products Adapt to Local Needs

As we talked to people managing global UX, we heard a lot of examples of ways in which their products had to adapt to local needs. Although many of these adaptations could be disregarded as just a small nuance in the scope of a whole product, it was also easy to see how they could be the difference between success and failure in a market. Often these stories came as an afterthought, after we were told that there really weren't many differences between countries. They included differences in:

- **How people expect to pay.** Credit cards, checks, debits and other systems vary both in how they work and in how they are used. In Brazil, Maren Pyenson says that the *boleto* system is the most common way to pay bills. All of your purchases are accumulated onto a statement, which people go to the bank to pay in person at the end of the month. In China, when making a hotel reservation, people do not expect to have anything charged to their credit card until they actually arrive, in contrast to the common practice in other countries.

- **The kind of information people want.** On hotel sites, different information can be more or less important, such as a phone number for those who want to make reservations in person, the types of photographs of the building and rooms, or how much detail the site has about the area around the hotel. During research on hotel booking in a South American country, Joe Leech found that users wanted to see photos of the bathrooms as part of the tour of a typical room.

- **What they use the product for.** A bicycle can be transportation to work or just used for play or sport. Does it need a basket to carry bags, or to be as light as possible; should it have tires for riding on city streets or on dirt tracks? Michael de Regt found this to be especially true for appliances. A rice cooker, for example, might be an everyday item in the kitchen or a special gift that is rarely used.

- **Perceived value of a product.** In research about sport in several countries Henning Fischer found very different attitudes toward running and running shoes. "In the UK, it was a bit boring, but there was a reward at the end. In France, it was something you do for beauty and wellness, and you don't pay much attention to the equipment. Germans run for mental well-being and balance in life. The Japanese had a strong goal, like running a marathon."

- **Communications style.** Katharina Reinecke found online credit card sites designed for the United States very different than ones in Germany. "We only trust info on banking sites if it looks very plain and defined. On American sites, they often have shopping links even on credit card sites. They make the whole thing untrustworthy because they are urging me to go shopping immediately. It wouldn't work that way in Germany."

- **Social interactions.** In a project in South America, Chris Rourke was surprised at how important social networking and testimonials were in building trust, but also learned that they had to be real. People in their usability testing were suspicious, saying, "Yeah, that's a story about how this person has benefitted, but I don't think it's real." You can't just roll the site out there and make up testimonials to pad it out.

- **Attitudes toward privacy.** There are strong differences in both laws and attitudes toward privacy, even within one region. A German participant in one of Bas Raijmakers's projects edited all of her photographs, cropping out faces so that no one could be recognized, even though there were formal confidentiality documents in place. In the United Kingdom, participants were much less concerned about pictures being take once the conditions for the user of the research materials had been made clear.

- **How the task is understood.** Cultural issues can change tasks that might seem very similar in profound ways. In Islamic banking, for example, Sharia rules on usury and interest change not just the conversation or perceptions, but the framework of making a large purchase like a house. Instead of the consumer borrowing money and paying it back with interest, the bank makes the purchase and leases the house to the consumer.

Knowing about these differences is not enough. You have to have local insight to understand how intertwined they are with local customs—and which ones are relevant for your product. Getting the details right opens up a whole world of opportunity that you might not think of, and getting them wrong can mean that your product fails for reasons you may not even understand because of how intertwined cultural, practical, and UX design issues can be.

> India, Brazil, Japan—people believe in taking turns, even if they are dying to say something, they will let you finish your thought. They won't cut you off. It's a more polite conversational style than in the US. They expect to be equally polite when interacting with a speech-based application and might not be willing to interrupt an instruction they don't need. When we are designing for a global product, we had to be sure to incorporate that into the design and be sure the team understood the cultural implications.
>
> **Jhilmil Jain**

Fit into the Local Environment

To create a good local experience, you also have to decide how to fit in (and differentiate your product) in the local environment.

Do you want to be part of the everyday experience, or something unusual and special?

> Chinese kitchens are small, so a rice cooker has to be small to fit into the kitchen, It's very difficult to achieve, and still be able to make enough rice for the whole family. You never know exactly how it will be used. Will it be a rice cooker given as a wedding present and never used again, or will it be the one used every day? Will your rice cooker be important enough that they will clear another appliance out of the corner to make a place for it? You also have to keep the brand perspective and local competition in mind. For example, if your competitor takes 10 steps to cook rice, you may decide that your product will do it in five steps, and be the simplicity brand.
>
> **Michael de Regt**

Many people mentioned the busy design of some Asian web sites with lots of movement and color on the page, and wondered whether this is a cultural trait or just a fashion. This question is about the line between custom and culture. That is, are differences in design a sign of differences in culture, or are they just differences? Customs may have started for reasons that have now been forgotten, and are continued through habit. They may emerge from the state of technology, or a social custom, or have been copied from the outside just as easily as from deep cultural values.

> The perception of Yahoo! is different in different places—it was very cool in HK, but by the time it got to SF, it was already old news. It's interesting that you could be the best thing in one region, but be totally discounted in the US. Orkut is a good example—it really took off in South America, but if you talk to people at Google about it, they can be surprised that it's still around at all.
>
> **Kevin Cheng**

One of the examples we heard a lot was the way many Asian sites have busy pages with more text and animations or movement, when contrasted to Western designs that are more sparse and have more white space. Kevin Cheng suggested that instead of "busy," people might see those pages as "fresh and exciting." Similarly, "sparse" might also be described as "clean and simple."

We also heard a lot of explanations for this: (1) Chinese characters are easier to read in a dense display than Western alphabets, (2) people in China are more used to seeing a complex information landscape, or (3) this is just the way design has developed in today's China and reflects the taste of people there.

Another example of a difference that falls in the grey area between culture and custom is the use of animation. When Sarah Bloomer worked on the Citibank ATM machines, they were designed in New York without any animation. Their design philosophy was that the interface would be conversational, but that there would be nothing extraneous to distract customers from what they came to the ATM to do. When they worked on ATMs for the branches in Japan, the local designers wanted to add an animation of the teller bowing. They had to decide whether to stick to the original design standard or add this local variation.

One explanation might be that the sites reflect the physical environment. In Hong Kong, for example, businesses aren't just

Figure 9.6 In 2004, there were at least six animated elements on the China home page. 1—4 are animated ads, 5 is a scrolling marquee, and 6 is a blinking indicator on the mail icon. http://www.uigarden.net/english/usability-half-way-round-the-world.

at street level; you get restaurants and stores and karaoke going up vertically for 10 or 20 floors in a building. Neon signs stick out from those businesses' windows trying to get attention. Was it designed that way, or did it just end up that way because Hong Kong is such a physically small area that space is at a premium and there was nowhere to go but up?

Daniel points out that what you are "used to" and what you "like" might be very different. "In our research in China, we've heard people say they like simple things." All of this points to the need to challenge and validate assumptions in global design through good research. Kevin suggested that you need to have the wisdom and understanding to say "I don't know everything." "It takes time to get to a point of saying that with peace and calm, but it will get you far, no matter what market you are designing for."

Design from Your Roots

This might not be an injunction, but something you can't help. We all work from our own experiences to some extent, but we also heard people talk about consciously bringing their own cultural roots into their design work to add depth. Both Wei Ding and Doug Wang created presentations to introduce their colleagues to Chinese culture and have spent time thinking about what this perspective brings to their own work.

Figure 9.7 Signs stick out from buildings on all stories in crowded Hong Kong streets. Steve Baty, http://www.flickr.com/photos/stevebaty/5463328584/in/set-72157626098311156/.

I'm trying to bring more cultural influences from my roots into my design work. I want to help my (Western) colleagues understand how diverse and sophisticated the Chinese culture is. In the West, we are always looking at how to conquer nature or advance humanity, but Chinese design looks for harmony and how to fit nature and society together. There are three perspectives.

First, social, which draws on Confucianism to help people learn to deal with one another.

Second, nature, where Taoism teaches that people are part of nature and should take the minimum to survive.

Third, the personal, and Buddhism, which helps people rethink their own position in life.

When we look at innovation, perhaps there is another requirement to find balance. As a designer, I have to balance eastern and western philosophy. When I think about how to create this balance, it helps me reintegrate my own life.

Doug Wang

DELIVERING VALUE

And so we come to the end of our journey. We have looked at why, and who, and how. But now it's time to look at how we leave the world better for our work and so add value to our projects, products, companies, teams, and the world.

We started this book looking for insights—and guidance—on how to "do" user experience in a global world.

The challenge we saw is this: User experience work rests on knowing our users. But when products, especially online products, can be used by anyone, anywhere, how do we stretch ourselves to stay true to that core principle?

If we had to summarize what we have learned on this journey, it comes down to this:
- In UX, we build bridges.
- As leaders, we have to set examples for collaborative global thinking.
- Everything we do should create value.

Build Bridges

Bridging the gaps between the product team and the culture, and context in which the product will be used, is the first responsibility for global UX.

> To be able to tell that story, for that project, we had to go there. We had to get to know Chinese people. We had to experience for ourselves. We had to do synthesis. We have to check in with people. And we are still seeing it. We don't yet understand all of the nuances of the differences, but we are seeing a convergence of values and trends and insights. We can bring that back as a story: Here's a slice of life in China, which is in a crisis for health and well-being. Here's a way it is different from a slice of life in this country. And here are some deep values we could potentially connect to.
>
> **Marc Rettig**

As we thought about this responsibility to make connections, we heard three messages:
- Any interaction with the people and context for whom you are designing is better than none. Whether your project has the

budget for extensive research and immersion or not, finding ways to do this work is critical.

- There are many ways to learn, and none is the "best." Each of us has to find the way to make the most of our own circumstances, skills, and personal preferences. There is seeing for yourself in deep immersion, quick visits, or local surrogates; and indirect information from research by others, local informants, or team members.
- Local knowledge is essential. No amount of research can replace a deep familiarity with the culture and context.

All this leaves us with a question: Is it possible to design (well) for a global audience without a diverse, global team that is open to innovation from anywhere? Is the killer reason to be global (as Jeff Eddings put it) that you bring together so many different perspectives and ways of seeing things that you can't help but have a richer product?

> Having different groups within our UX design practice helps us be successful. If you look at how we collect and share information with structured protocols, you could say our process is not so different from other companies. But because our teams are global, we have to be good storytellers, to tell how the design aligns with the business we are designing for.
>
> **Dennis Kei Yip Poon**

That's the underlying pattern. Knowledge and innovation come from everywhere, and to be successful in global UX, our teams have to be structured so they have ways to listen to all of those voices and can find the skill sets wherever they are located around the world.

> When I've gone over to India, to work with the teams there, I'm really impressed with their skills and their ability to ideate and come up with realistic, but innovative ideas. It's a switch. It used to be that the US team was coming up with more of these ideas. Now, they are coming up with the big ideas and we are doing the tactical ideas. In the US, we need to recognize them and continue to push ourselves.
>
> **Jim Nieters**

Sometimes the goal of a global team for global products seems to run up against the need to know a market well. Pabini Gabiel-Petit has worked on many configurations of global teams. For her, it's important that the UX designers are fully immersed in the culture for which they are designing

When you're creating a product to be sold worldwide, you need to ensure it serves the needs of users in your key markets well. Since your team members may not come from those places or be fully familiar with those cultures, the best way to achieve that is to do generative user research. In this case, your design team could be anywhere. But if you're creating a product for a particular market, you need to design it to meet the needs of users in that market. So it doesn't really make sense to have it designed someplace else. Ideally, at least the lead designer should be fully familiar with the culture. For example, the needs of users in Japan or China are very different from those of users in the US. Without designers' immersing themselves in those cultures over an extended period, it would be difficult to really understand their needs. So, at scanR, I worked with a team member who lived in Japan and a Product Manager who was from Japan to ensure we took the right approach when creating a product for that market. This is equally true for off-shore designers working on products for the US. It would help if they'd spent some time living in the US.

Pabini Gabriel-Petit

What matters is that the people who are doing the designing have a sympathetic attitude and are keen to explore and understand the users' world and environment. If you are not interested in your users, you are going to be an awful designer because you have to care whether the other person understands—and can own—the message in your design.

Giles Colborne

IMMERSION IS THE KEY TO CREATIVITY

"Although travel may indeed broaden the mind, the current studies suggest that deeper experiences such as living abroad are critical for producing enduring cognitive changes, such as enhanced creativity. Living in a different country may lead to the realization that every form—from gestures to vocal tones to a simple smile—can convey different meanings and have different functions depending on the cultural context. Those critical months or years of turning bewilderment into understanding may instill not only the ability to "think outside the box," but also the capacity to realize that the box is more than a simple square, more than its simple form, but is a repository of many functions and creative possibilities."

This quote is from an INSEAD Business School Research Paper, "Cultural barriers and Mental Borders: Living in and adapting to foreign cultures facilitates creativity." (Maddux, Galinsky 2007)

Lead by Example

Opening up to brainstorming by a wider group means letting go of some of our sense of ourselves as experts.

> As UX consultants, we are very clear that we don't know what we don't know. I'm always surprised by users and people and what they say and do. I wouldn't ever go into a project thinking I have all the answers. I've been caught out so many times in user tester before. Very different than a management consultant going in as an expert. That helps with the way you frame the questions when you are talking to the client.
>
> **Joe Leech**

Leading by example also means practicing for ourselves the behavior we want from the team and company. Give all team members visibility, so that they can share their insights and successes in an equal way (despite the challenges of communication over distance). We have to find ways to win what Kaleem Khan called "the battle between your own perspective and what your best instincts and training and experience tell you are the best ways to approach something to create the conditions in which people can have great experiences." This battle can be particularly fierce on a diverse team where there are many competing interests. "You have to know which elements are the important ones and which one you actually do need to stand firm on."

Kevin Lee suggests that we think beyond design, beyond user experience. Instead of trying to speak in the jargon of business, put our skills to use and build credibility through success on pragmatic projects the business cares about. If you start with projects that support the CEO's goals and deliver results, you can move beyond the same old projects and suggest new and innovative approaches. "One advantage of this approach is that you can start with the type of projects you have to do anyway. Use them to get to know the other stakeholders. But do those projects with a speed, with a quality of user experience, that will let you stand toe to toe and head to head with the global competition, from experience standpoint. You need a strategic view and projects to demonstrate your capability and vision. Having this patience is one of the things that separates the great designers from the good designers."

It would be easy to think that you are the expert if you were brought in to run a project in an area without a strong IT capability. Jennifer Carey did just that, working for element^n, a company based in Beirut, on a project for a Kuwaiti telecom company, to build a web site in the Sudan.

At first, I was really arrogant I thought I had all the answers, and that what I came up with would be better than my clients. But, we adopted a user-centered process. We started with the stakeholders. Getting all the executive stakeholders in one room together and sharing what was important to each of them stopped the project from getting blocked by any of them down the road. Then, we did their user research. In these tiny little storefronts, there were customers lining up out the door. The staff was amazing—really knew how to handle the crowds and how to describe the products well. It's a year after the project ended, and I'm more humble now. I thought we would bring a professional and enlightened view, but I see now that we are really facilitators. If I had to do it all over again, I would make it more collaborative, including customer support and people from the sales outlets from the beginning. They are the ones who know what is needed.

Jennifer Carey

Create Value

We need to understand the value at the heart of our work, so we can create more of it. Global knowledge and understanding are valuable.

In 2000, I was flying from Mexico City to Cairo and sitting with someone going to a major corporation's global sales meeting. I asked him if he and his fellow senior managers traded stories about what works in different places. He looked at me and he laughed at me and said, "Of course we do!" I told him that is so exciting because I come from a world of computer technology that is just learning about this topic. "There are so many people who would like to hear what you say. Would you be willing to be a keynote speaker?" He looked at me again and laughed again and said. "Of course I won't do that. Because all the things that we talk about are the closely guarded secret of our success. My company is 100 years old. Do you think we don't know what sells where by now? But I can share with you that we have analyzed it very carefully. And if we can see connections between say, certain locations in India and Brazil because of certain similarities between their situations, ...well, you aren't going to learn any of that!"

Aaron Marcus

One of the secrets is to keep asking questions. Drilling down through layers and layers of explanations. Jenna Date says that you have to ask the questions directly: "What's the value? What's the value to the user? What is the value to the organization? What is the value, period?"

> If you constantly ask yourself that over and over and over again in every research project, from my perspective it's no longer about building products for sale. It's about building products that have value to people and also have value to us as a global community. I don't think there should be a product made from this point on that doesn't attack one of the two issues of today: all the conflict that's occurring and all of the environmental change. What is the value at every step of the way when it comes to creating a peaceful, healthy earth?
>
> **Jenna Date**

Maybe the definition as simple as Tomer Sharon put it: "If I see that customers in all countries are happy I consider this as a big success."

We'll leave you with a last thought.

It's not just about creating great product experiences, it's something bigger.

Think beyond yourself.

Think beyond your team.

Think beyond the business or the organization that you work in.

So you can think about the whole user experience.

Whitney and Dan

REFERENCES

AM+A, 2001. Cultural Dimensions and Global Web Design: What? So What? Now What? [online] Available at. http://www.amanda.com/resources/hfweb2000/AMA_CultDim.pdf.

Andonian, A., Loos, C., Pires, L., 2009. Building an innovation nation, What Matters. McKinsey & Company. 4 March 2009. http://whatmatters.mckinseydigital.com/innovation/building-an-innovation-nation.

Bergiel, B., Bergiel, E.B., Balsmeier, P.W., 2008. Nature of virtual teams: A summary of their advantages and disadvantages. Management Research News 31 (2), 99—110. http://www.emeraldinsight.com/journals.htm?articleid=1669181&show=abstract.

Canales, K., Serota, L., 2010. Mobile mandate: Tribute to cultural connectors. Design Mind: Frogs on the Road—Frog Design, November 23, 2010. http://designmind.frogdesign.com/blog/mobile-mandate-tribute-to-cultural-connectors.html.

Castells, M., 1996. The Rise of the Network Society: The Information Age, Volume 1. Wiley.

Cervi, B., 2008. Finnish First. Engineering & Technology 3 (14), 66—69. http://ieeexplore.ieee.org/xpl/freeabs_all.jsp?arnumber=4659414.

CESifo, 2008. The effect of globalisation on Western European jobs: Curse or blessing? in The EEAG Report on the European Economy 2008; Europe in a Globalised World, EEAG European Economic Advisory Group at CESifo, 26 February Chapter 3 [online] available at. http://www.cesifo-group.de/portal/page/portal/ifoHome/B-politik/70eeagreport/30PUBLEEAG2008.

Chabukswar, S. (2007) Practical Approach to Usability Practice in the Offshore Development Space. Persistent Systems

Chavan, A.L, Gaffney, G. 2006. Design in India: an interview with Apala Lahiri Chavan. Information & Design, User Experience Podcast. December 2006. http://www.infodesign.com.au/uxpod

Child, P.N., 2006. Carrefour China: Lessons from a global retailer. Forbes.com, Oct 25, 2006. http://www.forbes.com/2006/10/25/carrefour-china-chereau-qanda-biz-cx_pnc_1025mckinsey.html.

Deutscher, G., 2010. Does Your Language Shape How You Think? New York Times, April 26, 2010. http://www.nytimes.com/2010/08/29/magazine/29language-t.html.

Douglas, I., 2009. Global Mapping of Usability Labs and Centers. CHI 2009, April 4—9, 2009, Boston.

Doumont, J.-L., 2005. Bridging Cultures: Segmentation, Strategies and Statistics. UPA 2005: Bridging Cultures, June 27—July 1, 2005, Montreal, Quebec.

Earley, C.P., Mosakowski, E., 2000. Creating hybrid team cultures: An empirical test of transnational team functioning. Academy of Management Journal 43 (1), 26—49.

Epstein, J., 2010. Global vs. Local Consciousness. Jer979 Blog—July 29, 2010. http://jer979.blogspot.com/2010/07/global-vs-local-consciousness.html.

Evans, S., 2008. Meaning is found in context. Applied Storytelling, May 31, 2008. http://appliedstorytelling.blogspot.com/2008/05/meaning-is-found-in-context.html.

Friedman, T., 2005. The World is Flat: A brief history of the twenty-first century. Farrar, Straus, and Giroux.

German, E., 2010. The internet's new billion: New web users—in countries like Brazil and China—are changing the culture of the internet. Global Post November 15, 2010. http://www.globalpost.com/dispatch/brazil/101112/internet-growth-web-traffic.

Giddens, A., 1999. The Runaway World: Globalisation. BBC, The Reith Lectures. http://news.bbc.co.uk/hi/english/static/events/reith_99/week1/week1.htm.

Gorlenko, L., 2006. The moment of truth: How much does culture matter to you? Interactions 13 (2), 29—31. [online] available at http://portal.acm.orr/citation.cfm?id=1116736.

Hagel III, J., Brown, J.S., Kulasoonriya, D., Ebert, D. (2010) Measuring the forces of long term change: The 2010 Shift Index. http://tinyurl.com/2aon8jl.

Hofstede, G., 1994. Business cultures: Every organization has its symbols, rituals and heroes. UNESCO Courier. http://findarticles.com/p/articles/mi_m1310/is_1994_April/ai_15630583/.

Hofstede, G., 2001. Culture's consequences: Comparing values, behaviors, institutions, and organizations across nations. California, second ed. Sage Publications.

Hofstede, G., Hofstede, G.J., Minkov, M., 2010. Culture and Organizations: Software for the Mind, third ed. McGraw-Hill.

Hsei, T., 2009. Your Culture is Your Brand. http://blogs.zappos.com/blogs/ceo-and-coo-blog/2009/01/03/your-culture-is-your-brand.

Iyengar, J., Chabukswar, S., 2008. Moving from Usability Oblivion to a Thriving Offshore Usability Practice. UPA. http://userindesign.com/Images/Papers/Moving%20from%20Usability%20Oblivion.pdf.

Kettle, M., 2010. Trapped in the Anglosphere, we've lost sight of next door. The Guardian, Posted August 19, 2010. http://www.guardian.co.uk/commentisfree/2010/aug/19/the-anglosphere-is-interesting-enough.

Khanna, Parag and Ayesha (2011). You Will Never Have to Study a Foreign Language. Big Think, January 1, 2011; http://bigthink.com/ideas/26386

Kolko, J., 2010. Connecting research and innovation with synthesis, Johnny Holland, December 10, 2010. http://johnnyholland.org/2010/12/10/connecting-research-and-innovation-with-synthesis/.

Larsson, A., 2003. Making sense of collaboration, in Proceedings of the 2003 international ACM SIGGROUP Conference on Supporting Group Work. Sanibel Island, Florida, 153—160. Nov 9—12, 2003, New York, ACM. http://www.mindswap.org/~tw7/temp/papers+refs/tagging/%5BLarsson%5DChallengeOfThinkingTogether.pdf.

Laurel, B. (Ed.), 2003. Design Research: Methods and Perspectives. The MIT Press.

Light, A., 2009. Designing for other cultures: Putting Hofstede to bed. Flow Think Blog. http://www.thinkflowinteractive.com/2009/01/14/designing-for-other-cultures-putting-hofstede-to-bed/.

Maddux, W., Galinsky, A.D., 2007. Cultural barriers and mental borders: Living in and adapting to foreign cultures facilitates creativity, INSEAD Business School Research Paper No. 2007/51/OB. http://ssrn.com/abstract=1021265.

Marcus, A., 2004. Insights on outsourcing. Interactions 11 (4), 12—17. [online] available at http://portal.acm.org/citation.cfm?id=1005261.1005270.

Markovitz, E., 2011. Adam Sachs, Kevin Owocki, and Dan Osit, Founders of Igniter Inc. http://www.inc.com/30under30/2011/profile-adam-sachs-kevin-owocki-and-dan-osit-founders-ignighter.html.

Munsch, K., 2004. Outsourcing design and innovation. Research Technology Management 47 (1), 27—30. [online] available at http://www.allbusiness.com/human-resources/workforce-management-hiring/744912-1.html.

Pisano, G., Verganti, R., 2008. Which kind of collaboration is right for you? Harvard Business Review, December 2008.

Polansky, A. (2006) Changing perceptions: Getting the business to value user-centered design processes. In: Sherman, P. (Ed.), Usability Success Stories: How Organizations Improve By Making Easier-To-Use Software and Websites.

Prahalad, C. K. 2009. The Fortune at the Bottom of the Pyramid. Pearson Prentice Hall

Prensky, M., 2001. Digital Natives, Digital Immigrants. In: On the Horizon. October 2001, 9 (5). NCB University Press, Lincoln.

Quesenbery, W., 2005. Usability half-way round the world UIGarden.net. http://www.uigarden.net/english/usability-half-way-round-the-world.

Quesenbery, W., Brooks, K. (2010) Storytelling for User Experience: Crafting stories for better design; www.rosenfeldmedia.com/books/storytelling.

Ranjan, M.P., 2011. Inclusive Design Invitation to Davos, Design for India. http://design-for-india.blogspot.com/2011/01/inclusive-design-invitation-to-davos.html.

Redish, J.C., 2004. Yours, mine, and ours: Connecting ourselves and the communities we belong to, Keynote at the Usability Professionals' Association Conference. http://redish.net/images/stories/PDF/YoursMineandOurs.pdf.

Rhiain, 2010. Younghee Jung on design research for Nokia. Nokia Conversations Posted August 19, 2010. http://conversations.nokia.com/2010/08/19/younghee-jung-design-research.

Sajeev, A., Raminwong, S., 2010. Mum effect as an offshore outsourcing risk: A study of differences in perceptions. Computer Journal 53 (1), 120—126. http://portal.acm.org/citation.cfm?id=1671659.

Sapienza, F., 2010a. Cultural Dimensions of Chinese and Chinese-American Websites Feb 3, 2010. http://www.filippsapienza.com/blog1/2010/02/03/chiamer/.

Sapienza, F., 2010b. Usability for Latinos. Filip Sapienza web site January 2010. http://www.filippsapienza.com/blog1/2010/02/03/usability-for-latinos/.

Saraf, D., 2009. India's Indigenous Genius. Wall Street Journal, July 13, 2009. http://online.wsj.com/article/SB124745880685131765.html.

Schaffer, E., 2006. A decision table: Offshore or not? (When NOT to Use Offshore Resources). Interactions, March+April 2006.

Schumacher, R. 2009. The Handbook of Global User Research. Morgan Kaufmann.

Seligson, H., 2011. Jilted in the U.S., a Site Finds Love in India. New York Times. http://www.nytimes.com/2011/02/20/business/20ignite.html.

Sherman, P., 2007. Connecting cultures, changing organizations: The user experience practitioner as change agent UX matters. http://www.uxmatters.com/mt/archives/2007/01/connecting-cultures-changing-organizations-the-user-experience-practitioner-as-change-agent.php.

Snyder, M., Sampanes, C., White, B., Hnilo, L.R., 2010. Creating richer personas: Making them mobile, international, and forward thinking. UPA 2010 Munich.

Spradley, J.P., 1979. The Ethnographic Interview, Harcourt, Brace, Janovich, 4.

Vanderbeeken, M., O'Loughlin, E., 2010. Sustainable change: Discovering motivations and building a community of values. Putting People First. November 25, 2010. http://www.experientia.com/blog/experientias-framework-for-behavioural-change-towards-sustainable-lifestyles/.

Vatrapu, Ravi and Pérez-Quinones, Manuel A. 2006. Culture and Usability Evaluation: The Effects of Culture in Structured Interviews. Journal of Usability Studies, Vol 1, Issue 4 http://www.usabilityprofessionals.org/upa_publications/jus/2006_august/vatrapu_culture_and_usability.html

Wadha, V., de Vitton, U.K., Gereffi, G., 2008. How the disciple became the guru, Global Engineering and Enterpreneurship. Duke University. http://ssrn.com/abstract=1170049.

Webb, J., Sharon, T., 2010. Engaging teams with rich reporting: Recipe for a research findings exo, User Experience. UPA. http://www.usabilityprofessionals.org/upa_publications/user_experience/past_issues/2010-3.html#webb.

Whitney, P., Kelkar, A., 2004. Designing for the Base of the Pyramid. Design Management Review 15 (4), Fall 2004.

CONTRIBUTOR BIOGRAPHIES

Peter Ballard
Managing Partner, Foolproof, UK
Peter is one of the founding partners of Foolproof, Europe's largest User Experience agency. Foolproof works with some of the world's best-known brands, in many cases working globally, to provide UX insight and Experience Design strategy for its clients.
Twitter: @ballyfool
Web: http://www.foolproof.co.uk/our-people/management-team/peter-ballard/

Robert Barlow-Busch
Partner, ArtBarn Partners, Canada
Robert is currently partner in a new breed of investment firm, helping start-ups build their business on a strong UX foundation. In a career of 16 years, he has kept "fresh" by working across disciplines and alternating between in-house and consultant roles. Robert has led the design of products in industries such as transportation, semantic technology, travel, telecommunications, and proteomics. His target customers typically span countries, if not the globe.
Twitter: @becubed
Web: http://about.me/becubed

Ronnie Battista
Executive Director, Experience Design, MISI Company (an NTT Data Company), US
Having worked in leading UX roles at Accenture, D&B, and Gextech, Ronnie is currently Executive Director of Experience Design at MISI. He is Program Director of the Rutgers Mini-Masters in UXD certificate course, where he also serves on the Curriculum Subcommittee for the Professional Science Master's UXD Program. Former President of the Usability Professional Association's (UPA) New Jersey chapter, Ronnie now serves on the Board of Directors for UPA International, leading global certification.
Twitter: @RonnieBattista
Web: www.misicompany.com

Steve Baty
Principal, Meld Consulting, Australia
Steve leads design teams in the research, strategy and design of products, services, and custom experiences for large corporate and government organizations. His work impacts the day-to-day lives of millions of Australians as they interact with education, financial, travel, and telecommunications services.
Twitter: @docbaty
Web: www.meldstudios.com.au

Jakob Biesterfeldt
Director of International Practice, User Interface Design (UID), Germany
At UID, I plan and manage UX research and design projects for clients all over the world. I established a global network of UX research partners to do multinational projects and research. To date, we have worked in over 30 countries on five continents. I've been working in UX since 2002. Before that, I made furniture and studied product engineering. I live and work in Munich. I play cello better than football.
Twitter: @jbiest
Web: www.uid.com

Sarah Bloomer
Sarah Bloomer & Co, US
Sarah Bloomer has designed user interfaces since 1986. In 1991 she co-founded the interaction design company, The Hiser Group, and helped establish user-centered design in Australia. Since 2002, Sarah was senior interaction designer at the MathWorks, Director of UX at Constant Contact, and principal consultant at Sarah Bloomer & Co often applying her global experience. She's delivered papers, tutorials, and workshops at conferences around the world.
Web: www.sarahbloomer.com

Kevin Brooks
UX Product Manager & Professional Oral Storyteller, Motorola Mobility, US
At Motorola Kevin designs and coordinates the development of new user experiences for the home electronics division, using stories as a vital element of his work. As a writer and performing oral storyteller, Kevin tells personal tales from his urban childhood, through to his present day parenthood and journeys through life. A stint at Apple during the non-Jobs years drove him back to grad school for a doctorate from the MIT Media Lab.
Twitter: @storykevin
Web: http://www.motorola.com/Video-Solutions/US-EN/Home

Andy Budd
Managing Director, ClearLeft, UK
User Experience Designer and CEO of Clearleft, Andy is the author of *CSS Mastery*, curates the dConstruct and UX London events, and is responsible for Silverbackapp, a low cost usability testing application for the Mac. Andy is a regular speaker at international conferences like The Web 2.0 Expo, An Event Apart, and SXSW. In May 2010, *Wired* magazine named Andy one of the top 100 most influential people in the UK digital sector, much to the pride of his mother and the surprise of everybody else.
Twitter: @Andybudd
Web: http://clearleft.com

Jennifer Carey
Director of Consulting, Element^n, US
Jennifer has more than 15 years of professional experience across diverse technical industries in the US, Europe, and the Middle East. With a background in technical documentation, functional analysis and user centered design, Jennifer has consulted with a variety of companies such as Siemens, Zain Telecom, and Nakheel. Most recently, as Director of Professional Services at element^n, Jennifer provided leadership and strategic direction to element^n's international consulting teams, defining the methodologies, standards, and processes used on client engagements, and providing targeted strategic and UX consulting on key client projects. Prior to element^n, Jennifer was Documentation Manager at Cerberus Dati, a division of Siemens Building Technologies based in Milan, Italy, where she set up and led an internationally distributed technical documentation department and usability testing team. Since the birth of her daughter, Isabella Christine, Jennifer has been on professional sabbatical.

Samir Chabukswar
CEO, Founder, YUJ Designs, India
Samir Chabukswar is the Founder/CEO of YUJ Designs. For over a decade, Samir has been involved in the design and management of 1000+ user experience projects across a variety of products and domains for many global Fortune 500 companies. Samir has set up and managed global, cross-functional UX teams and has played multiple roles—UX evangelist, strategist, designer, researcher and team leader—at the same time. Samir holds Masters Degrees in Human Factors and Business Administration.
Twitter: @schabukswar
Web: www.yujdesigns.com

Raven Chai
Principal Consultant, UX Consulting, Singapore
Raven has over 10 years of design and innovation experience. His passion in understanding how people search and interact with products and services led him to help businesses leverage design thinking to drive innovation. He has been the lead UX consultant for SingTel since 2008 and is instrumental in creating user-centric design culture into the organization, translating SingTel's business vision into actionable roadmaps and building an internal UX team.
Twitter: @ravenchai Facebook /ravenchai
Web: http://www.uxconsulting.com.sg

Calvin Chan
Mobile UX Designer, Genesix, Inc., Japan
After graduating with a B.Sc. in computer science, Calvin worked as a web software engineer and UI designer in Canada for 7 years. He gradually realized that people are the most important factor for a successful product, and his growing passion in delivering usable and enjoyable experiences led him to the UX design profession. Calvin moved to Japan in 2010 and is now working on UX design for mobile application.
Twitter: @calvinchan
Web: http://calvin-c.com

Kevin Cheng
US
Kevin is a global nomad who has settled into San Francisco after calling Vancouver, Hong Kong, Austin, and London home. A product manager and user experience veteran, Kevin was the product lead for the redesign of Twitter's web site, lead user experience and product at the gaming start-up Raptr, designed Yahoo! Pipes, and redesigned Cathay Pacific's web site.
Twitter: @k
Web: http://kevnull.com

Giles Colborne
Managing Director, cxpartners, UK
Giles is the author of Simple and Usable Web Mobile and Interaction Design published by New Riders in September 2010. Having worked in user centred design since 1991, he formed cxpartners with Richard Caddick in 2004 focusing on creating measurable changes to clients' businesses. Giles is a former President of the UK Usability Professionals' Association and now sits on their International Conference Committee. He has

worked with British Standards Institute in developing guidance on web accessibility.
Twitter: @gilescolborne
Web: www.cxpartners.com

Catherine Courage
VP, Product Design, Citrix Systems, US
Catherine Courage leads the Citrix Product Design Group, a team focused on driving design thought leadership and execution. Catherine's team is responsible for delivering exceptional user interface designs; driving user interface standardization across all product lines; and improving all interactions that create the customer experience. Prior to joining Citrix, Catherine was the Director of User Experience at salesforce.com. She co-authored the book *Understanding Your Users* and is an active publisher and speaker in the design community.
Web: www.citrix.com

Jenna Date
Director of the Masters in Human-Computer Interaction, Carnegie Mellon University, US
As the Director of the Master's Program, Jenna works with faculty, staff, alumni, and current students to create a rigorous, engaging, and rewarding experience for each incoming class of students. Prior to the Directorship at MHCI, Jenna co-founded Fit Associates, LLC. Fit's intention is to lead, nurture, connect, and equip conscious clients for the greatest impact for the common good. Fit's industry client list includes Nissan, Comcast, Whirlpool, SAP, Microsoft, and Respironics. Jenna worked with design, engineering, marketing, and executive teams to make their products and processes better for their end-users.
Web: www.hcii.cmu.edu

Janna DeVylder
Principal, Meld Consulting, Australia
Janna DeVylder is a principal at Meld Studios in Sydney. With over 13 years' experience as a designer and researcher in the US and Australia, Janna has led design teams and large-scale projects for agencies and inside higher education, publishing, financial services, government, and travel organizations. Janna is very active in the design community, serving as the President of the Interaction Design Association (IxDA), an international organization dedicated to advancing the discipline of interaction design.
Twitter: @jdevylder
Web: www.meldstudios.com.au

Bill DeRouchey
Creative Director, BankSimple, US
Bill is currently Creative Director at BankSimple, aiming to simplify how people interact with their financial lives. He previously directed interaction design at Ziba Design, served on the global board of the Interaction Design Association, and co-chaired Interaction 10. He is also often known as that guy who researched the history of the button.
Twitter: @Bilder

Dr. Wei Ding (丁卫)
Director, User Experience for Globalization, Marriott International, US
Dr. Wei Ding is currently leading the company's China e-commerce strategy effort and provides advice on the globalization and localization practice for the Asian markets. Wei has 19 years of professional experience as a user experience practitioner and researcher at various Chinese, US, and international institutions. Wei got her doctoral degree at the University of Maryland. She wrote about global UX design in her *Information Architecture* book, published in 2009 by Morgan Claypool.
Twitter, Sina Weibo: @wding777
Web: www.marriott.com

Matthew Dooley
Head of Digital Experiences, HSBC, Hong Kong
A senior strategic thinker and marketing professional with over 20 years' international experience driving change at two of the world's leading banks across three continents. Matt started out at ANZ Banking Group in Melbourne, where he was nominated for an international marketing award which brought him onto the radar of Hong Kong Bank, which he subsequently joined in 1995. He initially thought he would work in Asia for a couple of years and then head back to Australia, but he enjoyed the move so much, he has never returned. Matt pioneered HSBC's global Internet design standards.
Twitter: @mattldooley
Web: www.hsbc.com

Darci D. Dutcher
User Experience Designer, UK
After starting her career designing aircraft systems for pilot safety, Darci moved on to product management and User Interface Design for a number of products including project management and SOX compliance. In 2007 Darci joined ThoughtWorks as a UX

Designer where she has worked on numerous projects and domains across the globe. Darci has been instrumental in integrating effective User Experience Design into ThoughtWorks Agile delivery process. Darci recently completed a Masters Degree in HCI from UCL.

Jeff Eddings
Product Manager, StumbleUpon, US
A creator of web software, there isn't an aspect of making the Internet an entertaining, informative, and inspiring place that he doesn't like. And for the past fifteen years, he's done exactly that—both at big tech companies like Google and small but mighty start-ups like StumbleUpon.
Twitter: @jeddings

Hsin Eu
Director, HIE (Human Interface Engineering), Trend Micro, Taiwan
Hsin studied psychology, ergonomics, and HCI. She was in usability and design fields in the United States and Taiwan for the past 12 years. Hsin is now based in Taipei as a director in Trend Micro, one the largest security companies. She currently leads a talented group of UI and visual designers, developers, researchers, and technical writers. Her team handles a wide variety of security applications and online services supporting both consumer and business customers.
Web: http://www.trendmicro.com/

Will Evans
Director, User Experience Design, Semantic Foundry, US
Will Evans is Manager, Experience Design for TheLadders in New York City with 15 years' industry experience in interaction design, information architecture, and user experience strategy. His experiences includes directing UX for social network analytics and terrorism modeling at AIR Worldwide, UX Architect for social media site Gather.com, and UX architect for travel search engine Kayak.com. He worked at Lotus/IBM where he was the senior information architect, and for Curl—a DARPA-funded MIT project when he was at the MIT Laboratory for Computer Science. His passions include design and critical theory, information architecture, information visualization, and wine. He lives in New York City and drinks far too much coffee.
Twitter: @semanticwill
Web: http://blog.semanticfoundry.com/

Henning Fischer
Director, Amsterdam Studio, Adaptive Path, The Netherlands
Henning Fischer is the Director of Adaptive Path's Amsterdam studio and a designer. He moonlights as a strategist, researcher, and recreational sloganeer. He's designed for the page, the screen, the store, and the business process. He studied design at the Institute of Design in Chicago and the world at Tufts University. He travels from time to time. If he's lucky, it takes him somewhere new.
Twitter: @henningfischer
Web: http://www.adaptivepath.com

Pabini Gabriel-Petit
Principal UX Architect, Spirit Softworks LLC, US
For more than 20 years, at companies such as Google, Cisco, WebEx, and Apple, Pabini has set UX strategy and led UX design and user research for consumer and enterprise applications on the Web, mobile devices, and desktop. She designed the award-winning WebEx Meeting Center and Training Center, setting the industry standard for online meeting software. Pabini is Founder and Publisher of UXmatters and a Cofounder and former Director of the Interaction Design Association (IxDA).
Twitter: @pabini
Web: http://www.spiritsoftworks.com

Gerry Gaffney
Information & Design, Australia
Gerry runs Information & Design, a UX consultancy in Melbourne, Australia. He produces the popular User Experience podcast (www.uxpod.com). He's co-author of *The Usability Kit* (with Daniel Szuc) and *Forms that Work* (with Caroline Jarrett). He's a former managing editor of the UPA print magazine, *User Experience,* and continues to be an active board member. He has an interest in urban design and policy, though most of his work is in the online space.
Twitter: @gerrygaffney
Web: wwwinfodesign.com

Peter Grierson
Lead Experience Designer, REA Group Australia, Australia
Originally from Melbourne, Australia, Peters interest in ethnographic research and design sparked traveling and living abroad at an early age. Through his career, he has worked in internal

user experience teams and consultancies. Capturing cultural requirements of indigenous stakeholders in New Zealand was a recent and valued career highlight. He is a keen traveler for work and recreation, loving local cultural experiences. Peter enjoys cooking and jazz, valuing social and improvisational experiences in both.
Twitter: @usabilityninja

Adrian Hallam
Senior Technical Consultant, Global Publishing Services, HSBC, Hong Kong
Adrian has a degree in Computer Science and has over 12 years of technical experience in software development and consulting. His experience has been across the fields of IT, media, telco, education, and finance. Adrian is now working on digital publishing solutions for HSBC. He has a keen interest in software development, agile methodologies and being a part of enabling great user experiences.

Rachel Hinman
Senior Research Scientist, Nokia, US
Rachel Hinman is a recognized thought leader in the mobile user experience field. She is a Senior Research Scientist at the Nokia Research Center in Palo Alto, California, where she focuses on the research and design of emergent and experimental mobile interfaces as well as mobile experiences for emerging markets. Rachel is the author of *The Mobile Frontier: A Guide for Designing Mobile User Experiences,* published by Rosenfeld Media.
Twitter: @hinman
Web: www.rachelhinman.com

Dr. Jim Hudson
Lead Researcher, Global Customer Experience, PayPal, US
Dr. Hudson works with a small team of researchers who are responsible for all of PayPal's customer experience research globally. With fully localized web sites in 21 countries and 24 currencies, this requires working across many geographies, time zones, and cultures. Currently, Dr. Hudson manages researchers located in Paris, San Jose, and Singapore. Methodologically, Dr. Hudson's team employs a variety of tools, including qualitative and quantitative usability testing, eye-tracking, product experience surveys, and neuro-experience techniques.
Web: http://www.jimhudson.org

Jhumkee Iyengar
Principal Consultant, User In Design, India
Jhumkee is a UX Design consultant, mentor, presenter, teacher, and writer. Her 20 years in established and start-up organizations in India and the US have covered technical, consulting, research, and project leadership roles. She has conceptualized and taught UX Design at various levels, most recently, a design education initiative in rural India. Jhumkee has degrees in Industrial Design, Human Factors Engineering, and Mechanical Engineering and three awards and several publications and articles to her credit.
Web: www.userindesign.com

Dr. Jhilmil Jain
UX Strategist, Microsoft, US
At HP, I led an international ethnography study of netbooks in the education domain to understand commonalities and differences in regions to define opportunities for design of products, accessories, and infrastructure in those markets. Currently at Microsoft, I am leading international user research across Xbox, Windows phone, and Bing for speech. Our goal is to understand perceptions, barriers and facilitators of speech adoption across socio-economic segments to identify speech scenarios for international markets.
Twitter: @jhilmiljain

Kaleem Khan
Founding Partner, True Insight, Canada
Kaleem is a consultant, designer, researcher, and strategist. He creates great experiences and solves complex problems for start-ups, agencies, governments, and global leaders in mobile technology, consumer electronics, Internet services, software, healthcare, finance, telecom, and security. Kaleem advises Ryerson University, OCAD University sLab, and the Mobile Experience Innovation Centre. Based in Toronto, he leads Canada's largest user experience professionals' group. Kaleem is a frequent speaker at international conferences on UX, strategy, mobile, ethics, and social design.
Twitter: @kaleemux
Web: http://uxjournal.com

Anne Kaikkonen
Product Manager, Nokia, Finland
Anne Kaikkonen, PhD, works as user Experience Product Manager at Nokia's MeeGo organization. She has worked at Nokia as usability specialist, user researcher and in product

planning for 13 years. Mobile Internet services have been her main interest during the Nokia years. Before Nokia Anne has worked at Fujitsu Computers, ICL Personal Systems, and Helsinki University. Anne is involved with multiple HCI conferences, like MobileHCI, CHI, NordiCHI, etc. and makes peer reviews to multiple HCI journals.

Anjali Kelkar
Director, Studio for Design Research, Hong Kong
Anjali Kelkar is based in Hong Kong and runs her own design consultancy, Studio for Design Research. Her expertise is in conducting design research and translating the findings into design and communication strategies. She has published a number of papers on design research and been an invited speaker and panelist at several research conferences over the past decade. She is a graduate of Parsons School of Design and IIT - Institute of Design, respectively.
Web: http://www.studio4designresearch.com

Mike Lai
Visiting Assistant Professor, The Hong Kong Polytechnic University, School of Design, Hong Kong, China
Michael Lai is Visiting Assistant Professor at The Hong Kong Polytechnic University, School of Design in the Master of Design Program in Interaction Design. He received his BFA from Columbus College of Art & Design (2004, Columbus, Ohio, USA) in Advertising & Graphic Design. He obtained his MDes from The Hong Kong Polytechnic University (2010, Hong Kong, China) in Interaction Design. His research interests include the areas of design and technology, design and business, design education, and visual communications.

Kevin Lee
Senior Design Manager, eBay, Inc. US
A passionate global design leader with more than 13 years of developing award-winning UX solutions and brand strategies as well as cultivating and building a highly creative design team to deliver innovative products within a fast paced market environment. The professional experience includes social media consulting, consumer products, e-commerce, and healthcare & enterprise industry from companies and clients such as GE Healthcare, Whirlpool, eBay, Coca Cola, Harland, Bank One, LOWE, and other Fortune 500 companies.
Linked In: www.linkedin/com/in/kevinlee
Web: http://www.ebay.com/design

Joe Leech (红豆乔)
User Experience Director, CXPartners, UK
Joe has 8 years' experience working in User Experience in every continent except Antarctica. He's always surprised at how similar people are across the world and how everybody can't see that call to action regardless of the language they speak. He's worked with clients like Marriott, eBay, TUI travel, Kelkoo, and many others.
Twitter: @mrjoe
Web: www.cxpartners.co.uk

Sylvia Le Hong
User Experience Consultant, User Interface Design GmbH, Germany
Sylvia works as a user experience consultant and project manager at UID in Munich, Germany. Her main expertise lies in the user research and conceptual design of web and consumer products. She manages multinational projects and is author of a study about cultural differences and similarities in the use of gestures on touchscreen user interfaces. This research involved 340 participants in 9 countries and was presented at the UPA conference in Munich in 2010.
Web: www.uid.com

Yu-Hsiu Li
User Experience Director, Waveface Inc., Taiwan
I worked for two global companies before. One is a software company while another is a world-class hardware manufacturer. This working experience allows me to approach global users and understand how they think and behave. This prepares me to think glocally in UX design and research. Recently I joined a start-up. The glocal thinking helps me guide the team to design a global product locally and establish a global working culture.
Twitter: @yuhsiuli
Facebook: @yu-hsiu li

Tim Loo
Director of Consulting, Foolproof, UK
At Foolproof, I'm responsible for Foolproof's UX strategy planning practice. I've worked on many international UX design projects with multinational clients including Sony, Shell, Lloyds Banking Group, ABN Amro, and Investec. Prior to joining Foolproof I ran marketing, content, and editorial at one of Europe's biggest and most active investor web sites. I had a front seat for the dot.com boom and bust and learned valuable and painful

lessons about why building digital channels with customers (not just for customers) really matters.
Twitter: @timothyloo
Web: www.foolproof.co.uk

Trent Mankelow
CEO, Optimal Usability, Ltd, New Zealand
Trent Mankelow is the CEO and co-founder of Optimal Usability. He started out as a technologist, with a degree in computer science, but quickly found that his passion was in the intersection between people and technology. These days he spends a lot of time with New Zealand organizations trying to understand their customer experience challenges, and setting Optimal Usability's strategic direction. Trent regularly writes and speaks on customer experience, service design, and usability. He also helped to found the New Zealand chapter of the Usability Professionals' Association and served on its international board from 2008–2010.

Aaron Marcus
President, Aaron Marcus & Associates, US
Aaron Marcus, researches/designs user interfaces and cross-cultural communication. He is Editor-in-Chief Emeritus, User Experience; Editor, Information Design Journal; member, ICOGRADA Design Hall of Fame (2000); Fellow, AIGA (2007); and member, CHI Academy (2009). He has published eight books and 300 articles. Mr. Marcus is the world's first graphic designer to work with computer graphics. He taught at Princeton, Yale, UC/Berkeley, and the Hebrew University/Jerusalem. He is a pioneer in emphasizing effective cross-cultural UI design.
Twitter: @amandaberkeley
Web: www.amanda.com

Chris Marmo
Interaction Designer, RMIT University, Australia
Chris has worked in both Australia and Japan as an interaction designer and user researcher. He hopes to have obtained his PhD in Human Computer Interaction by the time this book is out!

Itamar Medeiros
User Experience Manager, AutoDesk Inc., China
Itamar Medeiros, from Brazil, currently lives in Shanghai, where he works as UX Manager in the Architecture, Engineering & Construction Industry Group at Autodesk® and helps promote

Interaction Design as coordinator for the Interaction Design Association (IxDA). As an Information Designer, he served on the board of the Brazilian Society of Information Design, and held a lecturing position as Assistant Program Director of the Visual Communication Department of Raffles Design Institute at DongHua University, China.
Twitter: @designative
Web: http://designative.info/

Jim Nieters
Senior Director of User Experience, Yahoo!, US
Jim Nieters is Director of User Experience at Yahoo!, where his goal is to make the experience a strategic differentiator for the business. Jim leads workshops regularly at Yahoo! and has taught the principles of leading workshops in many companies. He also writes a regular column on User Experience management and is invited regularly to speak at companies, universities, and conferences on innovation and leadership of User Experience. Jim has been a UX practitioner for 15 years and a UX leader for ten of those years. Jim enjoys being part of teams that deliver innovations that change market dynamics.
Twitter: @JimNieters

Noriko Osaka
Principal UX Consultant, Crossfrontier, Ltd, Japan
She has spent most of her career in international business, starting from overseas sales/product design assistant in a global manufacturer. She shifted her career to Web industry in 2000 and experienced such roles as a Webmaster in a US-based company, UX consultant, and Web Director in a major web integrator in Japan. She has both business and technical background, which serves for effective research and development in UX projects.
Web: http://www.crossfrontier.com/

Christine Petersen
Managing Director, Time Technology, Hong Kong
Christine Petersen, an authority on productivity and time management, is the founder and Managing Director of Time Technology. With a long and successful career in both learning and development and the corporate world, Christine has been at the forefront of helping leading individuals and teams in various organizations meet the demands of a constantly changing business environment.
Web: www.timetechnology.net

Martin Polley
Interaction designer, Intel (through IFN Solutions), Israel
An interaction designer, just trying to make the world a better place, one interaction at a time.
Twitter: @martinpolley
Web: capcloud.com and johnnyholland.tv

Dennis Kei Yip Poon
Chief UI Design Expert, Huawei Device Co. Ltd, China
Born in Hong Kong in 1968, Dennis left for England at age fifteen. After obtaining his MA in Computer-Related Design from the Royal College of Art, he has lived in the Netherlands, USA, Sweden, Belgium, Singapore, and China. His past professional experiences include working at IDEO as interaction designer, Icon Medialab as Process Coach, Philips Design as Senior Design Consultant, and Motorola as UI Manager. Dennis recently joined Huawei as Chief UI Design Expert.

Steve Portigal
Portigal Consulting, US
Steve helps clients to discover and act on new insights about themselves and their customers. He has interviewed hundreds of people, including families eating breakfast, hotel maintenance staff, architects, rock musicians, credit-default swap traders, and radiologists. Steve's work has informed the development of mobile devices, medical information systems, music gear, wine packaging, financial services, corporate intranets, and iPod accessories. He is an avid photographer who has a Museum of Foreign Groceries in his home.
Twitter: @steveportigal
Web: www.portigal.com

Maren Pyenson
Director, Product Management, BabyCenter.com, US
Maren has 15+ years of consumer product management experience and has worked at some of the largest global internet brands. As Director of Launch Management at AOL, she led the effort on the localization and launch of the first international AOL service in Germany as well as in France, UK, Brazil, Argentina, and Mexico. At Yahoo!, she was responsible for developing the "Front Page" international strategy in Europe and Asia. Currently, Maren is Director of Product Management at BabyCenter.com. Maren holds a BA in German Language and Literature (Minor: Japanese/ Political Science) from the University of Massachusetts, Amherst,

and has completed graduate studies in Information Systems at American University in Washington DC.
Web: www.babycenter.com

Bas Raijmakers
Creative Director, STBY, UK and The Netherlands
Dr. Bas Raijmakers is co-founder and Creative Director of STBY in London and Amsterdam. STBY is specialized in creative research for service design and innovation, and works for clients in industry and the public sector. Bas has a background in cultural studies, the internet industry, and interaction design. His main passion is to bring people we design for into design and innovation processes, using visual storytelling. He holds a PhD in Interaction Design from the Royal College of Art in London. He is also a reader in Strategic Creativity at Design Academy Eindhoven.
Twitter: @hellobas
Web: www.stby.eu

Michael de Regt
Senior Design Consultant, Philips Design Hong Kong,
Hong Kong
After finishing Graphic Design school and Interaction Design school I started to work at Philips Design Netherlands in 2000. The natural development over the years has been from Visual interface design to Interaction design in various Design studios, to currently Creative lead UX design for Philips' Consumer electronics in Hong Kong. I'm lucky that in my role I can use my curiosity and design passion to create meaningful innovations for the end-user.
Web: www.phillips.com

Katharina Reinecke
Postdoctoral Fellow, Harvard School of Engineering and Applied Sciences, US
Katharina Reinecke received her PhD in computer science from the University of Zurich in 2010, and she is now a postdoctoral fellow in the Intelligent and Interactive Systems group at Harvard School of Engineering and Applied Sciences. In her research, she combines the fields of human–computer interaction, cultural anthropology, and machine learning for an interdisciplinary approach to user interfaces that adapt their visual presentation and work flows to the varying preferences of people of different cultural background.
Web: http://people.seas.harvard.edu/~reinecke

Marc Rettig
Principal, Fit Associates LLC, US

Marc works with companies, institutions, and students to increase their positive impact on life. His 30-year career synthesizes design practice, systems thinking, immersive research, and social change facilitation, carrying him deep into the realities of life all over the world. In addition to his work at Fit Associates, Marc is a faculty member of the Masters in Design for Social Innovation program at the School of the Visual Arts in New York.
Web: www.fitassociates.com

Chris Rourke
Managing Director, User Vision, UK

Chris was born in the USA but mostly worked in the UK, providing human factors and usability consultancy. He established User Vision in 2000 and has led UX research and UCD activities in many industries, especially financial services, government, and e-commerce. He has conducted usability testing in Spanish and has most recently established a branch of User Vision in the Middle East, where cultural aspects provide a new dimension to the traditional UX challenges.
Twitter: @crourke
Web: www.uservision.co.uk

Tomer Sharon
User Experience Researcher, Google, US

Tomer is a UX researcher for Google New York working on Google Search and previously on Google's online advertising platform Doubleclick for Publishers. Previously, he worked at Check Point Software Technologies in Israel as a UX researcher. Tomer founded and led UPA Israel and he speaks in international conferences. His first book is titled, *It's OUR Research: Getting stakeholder buy-in for UX research projects.* Tomer holds a MS in Human Factors in Information Design from Bentley University.
Twitter: @tsharon
Web: about.me/tsharon

Josh Seiden
Program Director, LUXr, US

I am a user experience designer and manager with expertise working in entrepreneurial environments. I work with early-stage start-ups seeking design strategy, as well as with large businesses seeking disruptive change and innovation. Over 20 years working in technology I have developed specialties in

interaction design, service design, design strategy, and UX design in Agile and Lean Start-up environments. I have designed enterprise systems in complex domains as well as elegant, rich consumer experiences.
Twitter: @jseiden
Web: www.joshuaseiden.com

Maria Sit
Regional Managing Director - APAC, HeathWallace, Hong Kong
Over the past 16 years, Maria has worked with a number of financial services firms in different continents assisting them with communicating and living their brand promise. As a marketing and customer experience professional, the roles she played as an in-house staff and external consultant often varied, but the purpose has always been about bringing together the goals of business, customers, employees and the possibilities of technology to create greater value for the various stakeholders involved.

Vicky Teinaki
Interaction Designer, Locus Research, New Zealand
Vicky Teinaki is a Kiwi based in Newcastle upon Tyne where she is doing a PhD in Design at Northumbria University investigating the language designers use to understand touch. With experience in interaction design and product design, she is actively involved in the UX community as one of the editors of online magazine Johnny Holland. She can be found online as @vickytnz, where she's usually swotting up on British sci-fi or live-tweeting a conference.
Twitter: @vickytnz

Geke van Dijk
Strategy Directory, STBY, UK and The Netherlands
Dr. Geke van Dijk is co-founder and Strategy Director of STBY in London and Amsterdam. STBY is specialized in creative research for service design and innovation, and works for clients in industry and public sector. Geke has a background in ethnographic research, user-centered design, and services marketing. She is passionate about exploring the ways people co-produce their customer journeys by picking and mixing from multi-channel service touchpoints. She holds a PhD in Computer Sciences from the Open University in the UK.
Twitter: @hellogeke
Web: www.stby.eu

Michele Visciòla
President and founder, Experientia, Italy
Michele Visciòla is President and one of the founding partners of Experientia. Michele is an international expert on usability engineering, human–computer interaction and user-centered innovation. He has specific interests in new interfaces, notification systems, scenario design, and the usability-aesthetics relationship. Michele has participated in many national and international information system design projects, covering a wide range of expertise (from aeronautics to naval systems, and from internet to mobility systems).
Web: http://experientia.com

Doug Wang
Chief Designer, Pleasantuser Design & Technology, Ltd, China
Douglas has years of experience in graphic design, information architecture, user interface design, and design management. He returned to China to pursue an exciting career after living in Canada and USA for about seven years, In 2010, he started Pleasantuser Design & Technology to innovate tangible interfaces for 3D environments. From 2007 to 2010, he helped Autodesk China R&D center to build an international design team and manage more than six core products.
Facebook: douglas wang
http://wangxiaoyong.com and http://pleasantuser.com/

Mark Webster
Regional Business Development Director, Asia Pacific, JWT, Hong Kong
Born in England, I grew up in Hong Kong. Having experienced advertising in London during the 1980s I returned to HK in 1993 joining JWT. In 1997 I moved to Vietnam to establish our office as the country opened. I then moved to run our offices in the Philippines, followed by Thailand (with responsibility for ASEAN), followed by Japan. In 2010 I returned to Hong Kong in a Regional Business Development role.

Kimberly Wiessner
Creative Director, Customer Experience Technology, HSBC, US
Kimberly Wiessner is a deeply passionate user experience designer who has spent the past 6 years advocating for customers at HSBC. Driving a cultural shift within one of the world's largest organizations is no easy task, but Kim's respectfully relentless

customer-centered design approach has begun to make a measurable impact within the bank. Together, with her global team of colleagues, she is shaping the digital experiences of the future for the financial services industry.
Twitter: @kimwiessner
Web: http://www.hsbc.com

Jo Wong
Usability Consultant, Apogee Usability, Asia, Hong Kong
Josephine Wong was born in Dalian, China, grew up in Hong Kong since the age of six and completed tertiary education in Melbourne, Australia. She is the co-founder of Apogee Usability Asia Ltd. and has been in usability consulting and research in Asia for more than 11 years. In the past 11 years, Josephine has been practicing usability, research, and promoting customer-centered design in Asia. Jo holds a BS in Information Management from Melbourne University in Australia.
Twitter: @igiwong
Web: www.apogeehk.com

INDEX

Note: Page numbers followed by f indicate figures and b indicate boxes.

Check out our extensive list of titles in the area of UX/ HCI